THE VAGUS NERVE SOLUTION FOR HOLISTIC WELLNESS

SIMPLE PRACTICES TO RESET YOUR NERVOUS
SYSTEM, MELT AWAY STRESS, RELIEVE CHRONIC
ILLNESS, AND FEEL AMAZING IN YOUR BODY
AND MIND

DR. LEIA ANDERSON

The Vagus Nerve Solution for Holistic Wellness

Simple Practices to Reset Your Nervous System, Melt Away Stress, Relieve Chronic Illness, and Feel Amazing in Your Body and Mind

CONTENTS

MEDICAL DISCLAIMER

The information presented in this book is intended for educational and informational purposes only. It is not a substitute for professional medical advice, diagnosis, or treatment.

While every effort has been made to ensure the accuracy and reliability of the content, the Author and publisher make no guarantees regarding the outcome of applying the practices and suggestions outlined herein. Always consult with your physician or a qualified healthcare provider before starting any new health protocol, particularly if you are pregnant, nursing, have existing medical conditions, or are taking prescription medications.

The techniques described in this book—including but not limited to vagus nerve stimulation exercises, dietary changes, supplements, and lifestyle modifications—should be used under appropriate supervision and in the context of your individual health needs. Never disregard medical advice or delay seeking care because of something you have read in this book.

Use of the information provided in this book is at your own discretion and risk. The Author and publisher disclaim all liability for any injury, loss, or damage resulting from the use or misuse of the information contained herein.

INTRODUCTION

A LOVE LETTER TO YOUR NERVOUS SYSTEM

In today's fast-paced, achievement-obsessed world, stress, anxiety, and chronic health issues have become almost...normal. But let's be honest: just because something is common doesn't mean it's okay.

Right now, nearly 3 in 5 Americans live with at least one chronic illness. Many of them—maybe you included—have been told to "manage" it with medication. And while that can help, for many people, it's not the complete answer. The side effects stack up, symptoms persist, and that deeper sense of well-being remains out of reach. Visit after visit, doctor after specialist, the question still lingers: *Why aren't I getting better?*

In many cases, one significant root cause is hiding in plain sight: *chronic stress*. But how exactly does stress lead to so many physical problems?

Enter: *The Vagus Nerve*

This extraordinary nerve is the communication superhighway between your brain and your body. It helps regulate digestion, calm the heartbeat, ease inflammation, elevate mood, and much more. It's like the CEO of the rest, digest, and heal department... and yet most people have never heard of it.

That's precisely why I wrote this book!

Okay, truthfully, I almost named it:

How to Alleviate Basically Any Stress-Related Chronic Illness and Physical or Mental Symptoms That Arise from Stress by Activating Your Vagus Nerve With Amazingly Easy and Quick Daily Health Habits.

...but my editor gave me a look.

So instead, I give you:

The Vagus Nerve Solution for Holistic Wellness—a practical, empowering guide filled with the tools I've shared with hundreds of patients, now gathered in one place just for you.

You don't need a medical degree, a yoga certification, or a kitchen full of adaptogenic mushrooms to benefit from this book (though if you have the mushrooms, go you!). What you do need is curiosity, commitment, and a little consistency.

Even if you never make it into my office, this book is your invitation to experience the same transformational tools I give to my patients every day. In fact, many of them have told me they can still hear my voice in their heads as they stand in the grocery aisle, or pause before choosing between an evening walk or another Netflix episode (spoiler: choose the walk—then maybe watch one episode). My sincere hope is that my words will echo in your mind too, not as nagging, but as a loving nudge toward something better.

Because healing doesn't happen in one big, dramatic swoop.

It happens *bit by bit, moment by moment*. One nourishing meal. One deep breath. One body scan. One barefoot step on dewy grass. One stretch. One laugh. Yes—even one gargle at a time (trust me, it'll make sense soon).

WHAT YOU'LL FIND IN THIS BOOK

In these pages, you'll learn how to activate and support your Vagus Nerve—your body's secret lever for peace, clarity, and healing. We'll cover how it works, why it matters, and most importantly, *how to use simple, effective, science-backed practices to feel better.*

You'll discover:

- How to shift from 'flight or fight' into 'rest and repair'
- Easy daily routines to improve emotional resilience and reduce pain
- Nutrition, movement, breathing, and mindfulness strategies that truly work
- How small, consistent practices can transform your physical and emotional health over time

And if all goes well, you'll find yourself thinking, *"Wow, I didn't know that!"*... followed by *"I can do that!"*

DR. LEIA'S STORY

I grew up in the small town of Sidney, Ohio, where I was raised by my grandparents. My love for science started early, and by high school, I was fascinated by genetics and preventative medicine—fields that felt deeply personal after losing my mother suddenly to an undiagnosed heart condition, and watching my grandmother battle high blood pressure, chronic pain, diabetes, and eventually kidney failure and heart disease. I wanted a different path.

I earned my Bachelor's in Microbiology and then a Master's in Genetic Counseling. However, during my hospital rotations, I began to feel a growing sense of disillusionment. I saw what my grandmother had experienced happening all over again: patients being *managed*, not truly healed.

Late one night, searching for something more, I stumbled upon Naturopathic Medicine. Something clicked. I felt it in my bones:

This is what I'm meant to do.

Fast forward to today—I've been a licensed Naturopathic Doctor in private practice since 2013. My work focuses on whole-person healing: addressing the root causes of chronic illness and supporting each person's unique path to wellness with science-based natural therapies, lifestyle medicine, and compassionate care.

In my own healing journey, I've learned this work is as personal as it is professional. Despite doing all the right things, I developed SVT—a type of heart arrhythmia. My cardiologist's advice? Reduce caffeine. Manage stress. Stimulate the Vagus Nerve.

So I did. And everything I've included in this book, I've practiced myself. Today, I live in a state of calm far more often than fight-or-flight, and I want that for you, too.

This book is my offering—my way of placing a powerful, healing toolkit into your hands. Because you don't have to accept chronic stress, pain, or emotional burnout as 'just the way it is.'

HOW TO USE THIS BOOK

Read it with curiosity. Try the practices. Bookmark your favorites. Let it live on your nightstand or in your kitchen. Scribble notes in the margins. And most importantly, *put it into practice.* Because transformation doesn't happen by knowing something—it happens by *doing* something, consistently.

Whether you're here because of stress, illness, burnout, or just a deep desire to feel more like yourself again... I'm so glad you're here.

This is your invitation to reclaim your health and your joy, one breath at a time.

So let's begin.

With heart,

Dr. Leia

1

UNDERSTANDING THE VAGUS NERVE

Most of us are so busy keeping up with life that we don't often pause to think about what's quietly happening inside our own bodies. Between deadlines, dishes, and remembering to text people back, who has time to marvel at their nervous system?

And yet, tucked away beneath all the hustle is a true unsung hero: the **Vagus Nerve**. It's not flashy, it doesn't demand attention, but it's there behind the scenes playing a vital role in our wellness.

The Vagus (pronounced *VAY-gus*, not *Vegas* — although both can have quite an impact on your heart rate) is one of the longest and most influential nerves in your body. It weaves its way from your brain all the way down to the bottom of your gut, touching your heart, lungs, and just about every organ along the way. Think of it as a built-in communication superhighway, constantly sending calming, regulating signals to keep everything running smoothly.

You could call it the body's peacekeeper — the ultimate guardian of your calm. When it's happy, you tend to feel grounded, safe, and connected. When it's frazzled...well, that's when things can start feeling a little out of whack — emotionally *and* physically.

The Vagus plays a crucial role in maintaining what scientists call *homeostasis* — a fancy word for the body's way of staying balanced and steady, like a tightrope walker adjusting with every little breeze.

In this chapter, we'll take a gentle stroll (no cram sessions, I promise) through the basic anatomy and functions of this incredible nerve. Understanding it just a little better can help you befriend it — and believe me, it's a relationship worth nurturing.

Let's get to it — your Vagus is already excited. (Okay, maybe calmly anticipatory is more its style.)

ANATOMY OF THE VAGUS

The Vagus — officially known as cranial nerve X (10)- begins its journey deep within the brainstem, at a small but mighty spot called the medulla oblongata. From there, it sets off on an incredible adventure through the body, emerging through multiple tiny rootlets before slipping out of the skull via a passageway called the jugular foramen (yes, your body has all kinds of hidden doorways!).

As it meanders through the neck, chest, and abdomen, the Vagus sends out branches like a living, breathing highway system, connecting to major organs along the way — including your heart, lungs, and digestive tract. Imagine a vast, organic network weaving through your core, touching nearly every critical system that keeps you alive and well.

What makes the Vagus especially fascinating is its dual nature. It's composed of both **sensory** and **motor** fibers, enabling it to carry information in two directions — from the body to the brain and from the brain back to the body.

The sensory fibers are like scouts, gathering vital information about what's happening inside — such as blood pressure, heart rhythms, and digestion — and delivering those messages directly to the brain. Meanwhile, the motor fibers act on the brain's instructions, regulating heartbeats, stimulating digestive enzymes, and even relaxing smooth muscles when it's time to wind down.

This beautiful back-and-forth conversation is happening every second of every day, helping your body adjust to whatever life throws your way — whether it's a stressful meeting or a peaceful afternoon nap.

Evolution, being the master designer that it is, ensured the Vagus Nerve was built for survival. It powers the '**rest and digest**' response — the essential counterbalance to the high-alert state of stress. Without it, we'd be stuck in permanent overdrive. Thanks to the Vagus, our bodies know how to conserve energy, recover from challenges, and heal.

Among all the cranial nerves, the Vagus stands apart — literally. It's the longest cranial nerve, traveling far beyond the head and neck to oversee organs deep within the chest and abdomen. The Vagus sends motor parasympathetic fibers to all of our organs except the adrenal glands (the adrenals have their own role to play in stress adaptation by secreting hormones). While most cranial nerves stick close to home, the vagus ventures out like a true explorer, influencing systems far and wide. In fact, the nerve was first named for this quality; the word "vagus" is derived from the Latin word "vagari," which means to wander or roam.

The Vagus is a powerful reminder of how deeply interconnected we are — how signals from the brain affect the gut, how the heart's rhythm speaks to the mind, and how every system relies on the others to maintain balance. Even though we can't see it, we can certainly feel its effects every day.

As you progress through this book, you'll learn how to gently engage and strengthen this vital system, offering your body a natural way to handle stress and support healing.

The Vagus Nerve Pathway Through the Body

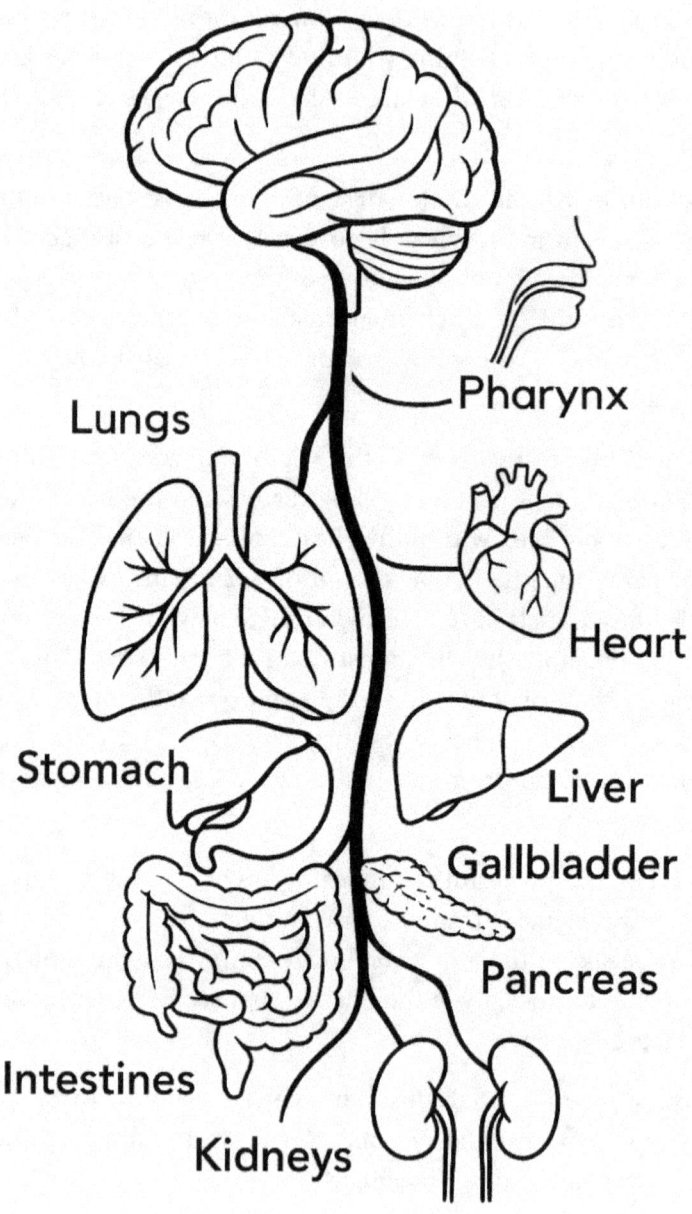

THE PARASYMPATHETIC POWERHOUSE

When life gets hectic, it's easy for our bodies to default to a state of high alert. Racing hearts, shallow breaths, tense muscles: the classic signs of the **sympathetic nervous system** kicking into 'fight or flight' mode. Thankfully, we're not stuck in this turbocharged state forever. Enter the Vagus — a silent supporter quietly working to bring us back to calm.

The Vagus is a major player in the **parasympathetic nervous system** — the part of our biology that tells the body, *"You're safe now. You can rest."* After a stressful moment (such as a tough meeting or a near-miss in traffic), it's the Vagus that gently taps the brakes, slowing your heart rate, easing your breath, and helping your body shift into healing and recovery mode. You might think of it as your body's very own internal peacemaker, helping you find balance again when life gets overwhelming.

On a physiological level, the Vagus wields remarkable influence over the automatic processes that keep you alive and well, all without you having to think about it. It helps slow the heart rate, promoting a more relaxed and efficient cardiovascular system. It stimulates the digestive system into action, ensuring that food moves smoothly through the gut, stomach acids are released at the right times, and nutrients are absorbed properly. You could say it's the ultimate dinner party coordinator — ensuring everything runs smoothly at just the right pace.

The Vagus also helps regulate your breathing patterns, keeping them steady and calm. It plays a crucial role in maintaining body temperature and metabolic balance, both essential for conserving energy and supporting overall well-being.

In the world of digestion, especially, the Vagus shines. It stimulates gastric acid secretion, encourages rhythmic contractions of the intestines (these are the *peristaltic* waves that move food along), and generally tends to the digestive garden with meticulous care. Whether you're savoring a five-course meal or simply trying to digest the events of the day, the Vagus is on the job, fostering a resilient and balanced digestive system.

But its influence doesn't stop there. The Vagus is also deeply involved in managing inflammation, acting through what is called the **cholinergic anti-inflammatory pathway**. In simple terms, it helps regulate the immune system's response, preventing inflammation from running wild. While a bit of inflammation is necessary for healing (i.e., how the skin around a cut becomes red before it heals, or how we spike a fever to kill off bacterial infections), chronic inflammation can pave the way for diseases such as arthritis, heart disease, and even certain autoimmune disorders.

For individuals with autoimmune disorders like rheumatoid arthritis, lupus, Hashimoto's thyroiditis, inflammatory bowel disease, or multiple sclerosis, enhancing vagal tone can be a game-changer. Studies suggest that enhancing vagal tone can lead to measurable reductions in symptoms and improved energy levels. Imagine reducing flare-ups and taming the relentless cycle of inflammation. Vagus stimulation may offer this relief by calming the immune storm.

When it comes to cardiovascular health, the Vagus again proves its importance. It affects **heart rate variability (HRV)** — the subtle variations in time between each heartbeat. A high HRV is a good sign, indicating that your body can adapt to stress gracefully and recover quickly. Through mechanisms like the **baroreceptor reflex** (tiny sensors in your blood vessels that help adjust blood pressure on the fly), the Vagus helps maintain stable blood pressure, shielding the body from the wear and tear of chronic hypertension.

Understanding the Vagus's role across all these systems highlights just how vital it is to our overall health. It's not just about feeling less stressed in the moment; it's about supporting the body's natural ability to heal, regulate, and thrive in the long term.

When we experience prolonged, unrelenting stress — whether mental, physical, or emotional — it erodes this delicate balance. You've probably heard the phrase, *"Stress kills."* It sounds dramatic, but there's truth to it: stress disrupts our ability to return to a restful, parasympathetic state, slowly straining every system in the body over time.

The good news? (And yes, there is good news!)

By supporting and enhancing the function of the Vagus — by nurturing our body's natural 'anti-stress' pathways — we can gently guide ourselves back toward healing. Strengthening the parasympathetic response isn't just about feeling better in the short term; it's about empowering your body's deep, innate wisdom to restore balance, resilience, and vibrant health from the inside out.

THE MIND-BODY CONNECTION: BRIDGING MENTAL AND PHYSICAL HEALTH

If there's one truth that ancient healing traditions and modern science agree on, it's this: the mind and body are in constant conversation. Far from operating as separate entities, our thoughts, emotions, and physical health are deeply intertwined, influencing each other in subtle — and sometimes not-so-subtle — ways.

Long before neuroscience caught up, systems like Ayurveda (an ancient Indian medical system) and Traditional Chinese Medicine recognized this dynamic interplay between mental and physical states. They understood that what stirs in the mind echoes in the body, and vice versa. Today's research confirms what these ancient practitioners intuited: stress, anxiety, grief, and other emotional states don't just stay locked in our minds — they ripple outward, shaping our physical health in measurable ways.

Acting as a two-way messenger, the Vagus facilitates a constant dialogue between brain and body, helping to regulate the delicate balance between mental experience and physical response. When you feel stressed, your body doesn't just *know* it — it *shows* it: a racing heart, shallow breathing, an uneasy stomach. Much of this physical response is driven by hormonal surges, such as cortisol, and it's the

Vagus that steps in to modulate, soften, and eventually help bring you back toward balance.

In more everyday terms: when you're anxious before a big presentation and your stomach is doing somersaults? That's your mind-body connection in action. When you feel your muscles relax after hearing reassuring news? Same thing. Emotions are intensely physical experiences, and the Vagus helps translate between these worlds.

Supporting this connection through simple, intentional practices — ones that stimulate vagal tone — can create shifts in your health over time. It's not magic; it's biology. Over time, nurturing your Vagus can help buffer you against stress, enhance emotional resilience, improve digestion, and even offer support for mood disorders like anxiety and depression. In strengthening this bridge between mind and body, we empower both to thrive more fully.

Real-world examples bring this to life:

Take one of my clients, a young professional grappling with chronic anxiety. Through regular Vagus nerve exercises, such as deep breathing, mindfulness, and cold exposure, she began to notice tangible changes: steadier heart rhythms, a calmer baseline mood, and a feeling of being more at home in her own body.

Or consider another patient of mine, a man with persistent digestive discomfort and constipation, who found relief through a combination of dietary changes and also tending to emotional stress through mind-body techniques. These stories remind us: when we address both sides of the equation — mind *and* body — healing becomes richer, deeper, and far more sustainable.

Another fascinating piece of this puzzle lies in the **gut-brain connection**, which is largely regulated by the Vagus. Science now tells us that neurotransmitters like serotonin — often dubbed the "happy chemical" — are mainly produced in the gut. (Yes, your digestive tract is basically moonlighting as a second brain.) The Vagus plays a key role in regulating this production and ensuring the lines of communication stay open. When we support gut health, we're also nurturing our mood, mental clarity, and overall emotional well-being.

As you continue reading and exploring practical Vagus strategies, I invite you to think of this work not as 'fixing' something broken, but as reconnecting what was always meant to be in harmony. Healing often starts by simply remembering that your body and mind are already on the same team, and strengthening that partnership through small, daily choices can create ripples of renewal throughout your entire life.

Reflection Section: 5 Signs Your Mind and Body Are in Harmony

1. **Calm Breathing:** Your breath remains easy and steady, even when stress arises.
2. **Smooth Digestion:** Your gut feels more settled, not twisted up by worry.
3. **Emotional Resilience:** Tough moments don't knock you down for long — you bounce back stronger.
4. **Lower Resting Heart Rate:** Your body signals, "I'm safe," more often than "I'm under attack."
5. **Quick Recovery from Stress:** You don't stay stuck in high alert; you return to calm more quickly and easily.

Overcoming Trauma with Vagus Support

Trauma can leave a lasting imprint—not only on the mind, but on the body as well. It disrupts emotional balance, reshapes thought patterns, and affects the nervous system in ways that can feel both invisible and overwhelming. Conditions like PTSD often emerge in trauma's wake, bringing symptoms such as flashbacks, hyper-vigilance, and emotional numbness. These aren't just passing discomforts; they can feel like living in a constant state of alert, as though your inner alarm system never quite gets the memo that you're safe now.

This is where the Vagus steps in, not as a magic cure-all, but as a reliable and science-backed ally in the healing process. Due to its direct influence on the parasympathetic nervous system, the Vagus plays a key role in helping the body feel calm and safe. By stimulating this nerve, we encourage the body to exit its high-alert state and enter a state of rest, repair, and recovery. Think of it like dimming the lights after a long, overstimulating day—it creates the right conditions for healing to begin.

Many Vagus exercises can be beneficial for those recovering from trauma. One such technique is **body scan meditation** (discussed in more detail in Chapter 8), which gently guides your awareness through various parts of the body. This kind of mindfulness fosters a connection to the physical self, something that trauma often disrupts. Tuning into physical sensations without judgment can help you feel more anchored in the present moment, reducing dissociation and bringing a greater sense of stability.

Another useful tool is **bilateral stimulation**—a technique that engages both sides of the brain, often used in trauma therapy (like EMDR). You can try it at home by lightly tapping each knee in an alternating rhythm or listening to audio tracks that shift from one ear to the other. These gentle, rhythmic actions can support emotional regulation and help the brain process experiences more fully, while also stimulating the Vagus in the process.

As always, healing from trauma is personal. It's not linear. But each moment you spend tending to your nervous system is an act of self-care, self-trust, and transformation. Use these tools as you're ready, and let them remind you: you're not broken—you're healing.

THE DOWNSHIFT: WHY VAGUS ACTIVITY DECREASES

To understand why the Vagus sometimes struggles to do its job, we need to zoom out and look at the bigger picture, specifically the mental and physical stressors that wear it down over time.

Emotional stress is a major player. Past traumas, ongoing anxieties, perfectionism, toxic relationships, and even the endless to-do lists we glorify can all keep the nervous system stuck in overdrive. When the mind is constantly bracing for impact, the Vagus can get worn out, like a computer trying (and failing) to run a hundred tabs at once. Eventually, things start to slow down, glitch, or just plain crash.

Physical stressors also join the party. Alignment matters more than we realize, especially the bones of the skull and neck, where the Vagus takes its first steps on its long journey. Misalignments can occur early (even at birth) or later through injuries such as whiplash or the gradual development of poor posture. Picture the Vagus as a vital cable threading through the body. If the framework around it shifts— even slightly—the whole system can get pinched or jammed, affecting everything downstream.

Proper nutrition is also essential. Our nerves depend on specific nutrients, especially B Vitamins, to stay strong and resilient. A diet lacking whole foods may lead to vitamin deficiencies that prevent our nervous system from functioning optimally. Similarly, overindulgence in processed foods can introduce pro-inflammatory sugars, oils, and synthetic food additives that harm nerve cells (and all types of cells in the body, for that matter).

Sleep is equally crucial; without deep rest, the body's repair systems can't function properly. And then there are toxins—the invisible saboteurs. From pesticides to household cleaners, our modern world is filled with substances that can quietly damage nerve tissue. The good news? Many exposures are optional once we start paying attention to what we bring into our homes, put on our skin, and put on our plates.

Another stealthy culprit? Blood sugar. High levels of glucose, especially when persistent, can damage nerves over time. Think of it like a wire cable that's frayed from constant strain—it eventually loses its strength and signal clarity.

When the Vagus falters, it's rarely because of just one thing. More often, it's a collection of little stressors piling up like bricks. But here's the hopeful part: every small positive shift—whether it's stretching more, eating better, sleeping deeper, breathing slower—helps lift the weight off the Vagus and gives it space to heal.

CONDITIONS ASSOCIATED WITH VAGUS DYSFUNCTION

As you've probably gathered by now, the Vagus wears many hats—and when it's not functioning at its best (what we might call "under stimulated," or simply overwhelmed), the ripple effects can show up in surprising ways. Because it plays such a pivotal role in regulating critical systems, a wide range of symptoms and health conditions can be traced back to Vagus dysfunction. Here's a look at some of the common issues that may be linked to a Vagus that's struggling to keep up:

- **Brain, Mental, and Emotional symptoms/disorders:**
  - Addictive tendencies
  - Anxiety
  - Attention-deficit and hyperactive disorder (ADHD)
  - Brain fatigue or 'brain fog'
  - Compulsive disorders
  - Dementia
  - Depression
  - Difficulty making decisions
  - Epilepsy (seizures)
  - Excessive worrying
  - Fearfulness
  - Feeling of heaviness
  - Feeling stressed
  - Hopelessness
  - Irritability or anger
  - Impaired cognition or poor memory
  - Restlessness
  - Sense of Impending doom

- **Body symptoms/disorders:**
  - Abdominal bloating, cramping, or pain
  - Allergies
  - Autoimmune disorders
  - Asthma
  - Blood pressure is too high or too low
  - Chronic fatigue
  - Chronic pain
  - Cold hands and feet
  - Constipation
  - Dizziness
  - Fibromyalgia
  - Grinding teeth or jaw clenching
  - Headaches or migraines
  - Excessive stress response (excess sweating)
  - Gallbladder dysfunction
  - Immune dysregulation
  - Insomnia
  - Irregular heartbeat
  - Irritable bowel syndrome (IBS)
  - Mast cell activation syndrome
  - Palpitations
  - Postural orthostatic tachycardia syndrome (POTS)
  - Small intestinal bacterial overgrowth (SIBO)
  - Systemic inflammation

Dysfunction in the Vagus can manifest as mental strain, often leading to increased anxiety or depressive states. It's like a radio antenna receiving mixed signals, unable to provide a clear signal. In such cases, people's lives may feel overwhelmed by excessive worrying or persistent brain fog. Decision-making becomes a daunting task, and fearfulness can cloud judgment. The emotional weight of these conditions can be profound, often leading to isolation or despair. The nerve's role in emotional regulation means its dysfunction can exacerbate feelings of hopelessness or irritability.

On a physical level, Vagus nerve issues can lead to systemic symptoms that disrupt daily life. Imagine dealing with chronic fatigue, where each step feels like walking through sand. Or experiencing persistent abdominal pain that no amount of diet change seems to alleviate. Blood pressure fluctuations may leave you lightheaded, while irregular heartbeats cause palpitations that set your anxiety on edge. The nerve's influence on immune response can trigger allergies or autoimmune flare-ups, leading to a cycle of inflammation and discomfort.

The connection between the mind and body is undeniable. Those with Vagus dysfunction might find themselves trapped in a cycle where mental stress causes physical symptoms, which in turn amplify mental strain. It's a feedback loop that can feel endless. But understanding this connection is the first step in breaking the cycle. Recognizing the interconnection between mental and physical symptoms offers a path toward healing and balance.

2

THE SCIENCE BEHIND THE
VAGUS NERVE

NEUROPLASTICITY AND THE VAGUS

I magine your brain as a living landscape—constantly growing, shifting, and reshaping itself in response to your experiences. This incredible adaptability is called **neuroplasticity**, and it's one of the brain's most powerful tools. Neuroplasticity is what allows us to learn new skills, form memories, adapt to changes, and even recover after injuries. Far from being static, your brain is vibrant and alive, continuously evolving to meet the demands of life.

One fascinating aspect of this adaptability is how closely it's tied to the Vagus. Stimulating the Vagus has been shown to enhance neuroplasticity, helping the brain forge new and stronger connections between neurons. Think of these neural pathways like well-worn trails through a forest; the more they're used, the stronger and faster they become. Vagus stimulation also promotes **neurogenesis** (the birth of new neurons), especially in places like the hippocampus, a region critical for memory, learning, and emotional regulation. It's like planting seeds in a garden: with the right conditions, they grow into a lush, thriving ecosystem.

The therapeutic potential here is great. For individuals recovering from events like strokes or traumatic brain injuries, Vagus stimulation offers a novel tool to support healing. It can encourage the brain to reorganize itself, forming new pathways that compensate for areas that may have been damaged. In stroke rehabilitation, for instance, patients have shown improvements in regaining motor skills and cognitive functions when Vagus stimulation is paired with therapy. Similarly, after a traumatic brain injury, it can help rebuild the neural groundwork necessary for clearer thinking and emotional resilience.

Reflection Section: Your Brain's Resilience

Take a moment to think about a time when you had to learn something completely new—maybe a new job, a new language, or adapting to a significant life change. How did that process feel for you? Were there moments of frustration followed by sudden clarity? That's neuroplasticity in action: your brain flexing, stretching, and building new pathways.

Recognizing your brain's natural ability to adapt is a powerful insight. As you'll discover throughout this book, supporting your Vagus is one way to help maintain that adaptability, creating a foundation for healing, growth, and lifelong learning.

DEMYSTIFYING VAGAL TONE AND ITS IMPORTANCE

Imagine your body as a finely tuned orchestra, each instrument playing its part in perfect harmony. Now imagine the Vagus as the conductor—subtle, powerful, and essential for keeping the music flowing smoothly. That underlying rhythm? That's your **vagal tone**: a reflection of how effectively your Vagus regulates key functions like heart rate, digestion, and emotional balance.

High vagal tone is a sign that your body's nervous system is adaptable and resilient. It's like having a conductor who can effortlessly switch from a dramatic symphony to a light-hearted waltz, helping you move from stress back to relaxation with ease. Low vagal tone, on the other hand, signals a system under siege—struggling to manage stress, regulate inflammation, or bounce back after setbacks.

Chronic stress, unfortunately, is like throwing the orchestra into disarray: the violins screech, the drums pound uncontrollably, and the conductor is nowhere to be found. Over time, ongoing stress acts like a slow, relentless drain on your battery, wearing down your vagal tone and leaving you more vulnerable to illness, emotional burnout, and chronic disease.

Research ties low vagal tone to higher inflammation, weakened immune response, heart disease, digestive troubles, and even mental health issues like depression and anxiety. It's as if the body's internal 'weather system' shifts from sunny skies to a permanent state of gloomy drizzle. Meanwhile, robust vagal tone supports everything from fewer colds to better blood sugar control, and even a longer, healthier life. Continuing with our weather metaphor (because, by now, I'm sure you've noticed I love a good metaphor!), when vagal tone is strong, life's inevitable storms pass through without leaving destruction in their wake. When it's weak, even a light rain can cause a flood.

The good news? You're not powerless here. Vagal tone is not a fixed trait—you can nurture it, strengthen it, and rebuild your resilience with simple, intentional practices. Strengthening your Vagus could very well be one of the most important (and most overlooked) strategies for living a healthier, more vibrant life.

THE SCIENCE SPEAKS: CUTTING-EDGE RESEARCH

The field of Vagus research is already impressive—and it's just warming up. Over the past few decades, a wave of landmark studies has illuminated just how deeply this nerve influences our mental, emotional, and physical health.

For starters, double-blind studies consistently show that **Vagus Nerve stimulation (VNS)** can lower stress-related symptoms. Participants who engaged in stimulation experienced not only subjective relief but also measurable drops in stress biomarkers. It's not wishful thinking —it's cold, hard data.

One particularly groundbreaking finding: a direct link between heart rate variability (HRV) and vagal tone. Individuals with higher vagal tone didn't just feel better—they actually *weathered stress better*, recovering more quickly and maintaining stronger cardiovascular health over time.

When it comes to anxiety and depression, the story gets even more compelling. Numerous studies have found that individuals struggling with anxiety disorders tend to show lower vagal tone, suggesting a biological underpinning to their emotional struggles, not just a 'mind over matter' situation. And for those with treatment-resistant depression, VNS has opened new doors. Patients who hadn't responded to conventional treatments found remarkable improvements with vagal stimulation.

The benefits don't stop there. Clinical trials have shown that VNS can help reduce the frequency of epileptic seizures. Other studies suggest that stress can lead to faster emotional recovery, sharper improvements in memory and attention, and even relief from chronic pain. This nerve plays a remarkable role in modulating pain, acting as a natural pain relief pathway. By stimulating the Vagus, you can tap into your body's innate ability to alleviate discomfort. This nerve doesn't just dull pain; it alters how you perceive it. When the Vagus is engaged, your tolerance to pain increases, providing a sense of control and relief. This modulation helps break the cycle of pain and its emotional ramifications, offering a path to reclaiming your life from chronic agony.

Even more exciting, non-invasive Vagus stimulation is now a reality. Gone are the days of thinking nerve stimulation meant invasive surgery; today, innovative devices deliver gentle electrical impulses through the skin. Early evidence shows these methods are not just effective, but easily accessible, offering potential help for conditions like fibromyalgia, autoimmune diseases, and other chronic illnesses.

Importantly, this isn't flimsy, early-stage science. The methodologies are rock-solid: clinical trials with rigorous controls, careful statistical analyses to rule out random chance, and peer-reviewed publications in reputable journals such as *Nature* and *The Lancet*. Leading neuro-science centers continue to push the boundaries of what we know—and what's possible. To see for yourself, PubMed Central (PMC) has a free full-text archive of biomedical and life sciences journal literature at the U.S. National Institutes of Health's National Library of Medicine (NIH/NLM). Just go to: pmc.ncbi.nlm.nih.gov/. Type "vagus nerve" into the search bar, and scroll through 100s of amazing articles.

In short, science has our back. As research deepens, the Vagus continues to prove itself as a powerfully versatile ally in the pursuit of health and healing. Whether it's stress, emotional resilience, cognitive vitality, or managing chronic illness, the evidence consistently points to the same conclusion: *supporting your Vagus Nerve means supporting your whole self.* As I like to say, "Heal the root, heal the whole."

The Impact of Ongoing Research on Healthcare

We're on the cusp of a transformation in healthcare—one where science is helping shift the medical model from a reactive to a proactive approach. Traditionally, healthcare has focused on managing illness after symptoms arise. But what if we could intervene earlier, using tools that support nervous system regulation to help prevent stress-related conditions before they even manifest?

That's exactly the potential emerging from current research on vagal tone. As we integrate Vagus care into preventive medicine frameworks, we move toward a system that values wellness as much as it does disease treatment. Supporting vagal health could soon become a standard component of chronic illness management, particularly for conditions driven by inflammation.

At the same time, breakthroughs in genetic research are shedding light on how individual genetic variations affect vagal responsiveness. This opens the door to **precision medicine**—care that's genetically tailored and personalized. Understanding how your genes influence your health risks may help your doctor recommend specific breathing practices, supplements, or therapies that are uniquely suited to your physiology.

The Future of Integrative Health

As we look ahead, the possibilities for Vagus wellness are as exciting as they are expansive. The growing partnership between traditional medicine and integrative health models is already creating a richer, more collaborative approach to care.

Imagine a future where your naturopathic doctor and your primary care physician collaborate, combining modern diagnostics and pharmaceuticals with time-honored therapies such as acupuncture, breathwork, herbal medicine, and somatic release. The result? *Truly holistic care* that supports body, mind, and spirit. This is what I have always strived to offer my clients… so I guess the future is now!

Artificial Intelligence is also entering this space, helping practitioners interpret vast amounts of health data and identify trends that can refine treatment protocols. With AI's help, we may soon be able to create customized Vagus care plans that adapt to each individual's genetic makeup, daily stress levels, and long-term health goals.

As all of these innovations evolve, one thing remains clear: collaboration between disciplines will be key. Each tradition—whether clinical, naturopathic, or ancestral—brings something essential to the table. Together, they help paint a fuller picture of what ideal holistic health care can look like.

How You Can Get Involved in Research

Curious about contributing to the next wave of medical breakthroughs? You can be part of the discovery.

- **Participate in Clinical Trials** – Many trials welcome participants with conditions like anxiety, depression, or chronic inflammation. Find opportunities through local hospitals, clinicaltrials.gov, researchmatch.org, or clinicaltrialsregister.eu

- **Join Research Registries** – Help researchers by sharing your health data in secure, anonymized databases that fuel studies. Find out more at the National Institutes of Health web page: nih.gov/health-information/nih-clinical-research-trials-you/list-registries
- **Follow and Support Research Institutions** – Stay informed through newsletters or social media channels from organizations studying neuroscience, longevity, and integrative health. For example, Society for Neuroscience (sfn.org), brainfacts.org, bluezones.com, The Institute for Functional Medicine (ifm.org), and naturopathic.org.

Your involvement isn't just helpful, it's powerful. You could help refine treatments and expand access to safe, evidence-informed care for thousands of others.

By staying curious, engaged, and open to this evolving science, you're not just investing in your health—you're helping shape the future of medicine.

ACHIEVING LONGEVITY THROUGH VAGAL HEALTH

It may go without saying, but I'll say it anyway: anything that boosts your health and reduces chronic illness will naturally support longevity.

Strong vagal tone has been linked to reduced risk of chronic illnesses that tend to tag along with age, including heart disease, diabetes, and cognitive decline. Think of it as tuning up the body's internal systems so they hum along smoothly, rather than sputtering with wear and tear. The Vagus supports this harmony by regulating inflammation, improving circulation and digestion, and helping the body manage stress, key players in how gracefully we age.

And speaking of graceful aging, let's talk brain health. One of the Vagus Nerve's lesser-known talents is enhancing blood flow to the brain while helping to reduce neuroinflammation. In simpler terms, it helps keep your mind clear and focused, which is pretty useful when you want to remember where you left your reading glasses… or why you walked into the kitchen. This nervous system support helps keep your mind clear and sharp as the years go by.

But longevity isn't just about the number of birthdays—it's about how you feel living them. Vagal health helps maintain mobility and flexibility, making everyday tasks like climbing stairs, gardening, or chasing grandchildren feel easier and more joyful. Regular stimulation of the Vagus has even been shown to support muscle tone and joint function, helping you stay active and engaged.

And of course, as already mentioned, a well-toned Vagus helps keep your heart rate stable and blood pressure balanced. It's one of the reasons vagal function is increasingly studied in the field of gerontology—the science of aging—with encouraging results.

So, how do you keep your Vagus youthful? Start with regularly following the simple guidelines outlined throughout this book. Longitudinal research confirms that people with higher vagal tone tend to be more resilient to stress and live longer, healthier lives. The science is clear: supporting your Vagus may be one of the most natural and effective ways to promote graceful aging and protect quality of life.

Aging with vitality doesn't require perfect genes or extreme discipline. It starts with small, consistent practices that support the body's built-in ability to self-regulate and heal. When you tend to your Vagus, you're investing in more than just a longer life—you're investing in a richer, more connected, and more vibrant one.

BUILDING RESILIENCE BY ENHANCING VAGAL TONE

Resilience. The beautiful quality that lets you take a punch (or twelve) from life and still get back up, straighten your crown, and keep moving forward. It's not about avoiding storms, it's about learning to dance (or at least stay upright) when the winds pick up.

At its core, **resilience** is your ability to navigate stress without losing your spark. A strong Vagus helps regulate your stress responses, so that after a challenge, your body and mind can return to a calm, stable state instead of getting stuck in high-alert mode.

Picture it this way: resilience isn't just grit—it's also flexibility. It's your internal GPS recalculating after every wrong turn or unexpected detour. And vagal tone is the invisible co-pilot, whispering directions, encouraging you to take a deep breath, and reminding you there's still a scenic route ahead.

Enhancing vagal tone strengthens this internal flexibility. It moderates the rush of stress hormones, steadies your heartbeat, and helps your body return to a rest-and-repair state more quickly. Instead of living at the mercy of every email, traffic jam, or unexpected life plot twist, you move through the chaos with more grace—and much less collateral damage.

Up next, we'll delve into practical vagal exercises, including breathing techniques, cold exposure practices, mindfulness rituals, and more. You can implement these simple practices to weave more resilience into your life starting *today*!

3

VAGUS STIMULATION TECHNIQUES TO ELEVATE YOUR VITALITY

Within you lies a built-in gateway to greater calm, resilience, and vitality—the Vagus. And the best part? You don't need expensive equipment, complicated rituals, or endless appointments to access its power. You already carry the tools you need in your own body.

In this chapter, we'll explore simple, science-backed practices you can incorporate into your daily life, starting with the breath and expanding into the transformative vibrations of humming, singing, gargling, laughter, sound therapy, and the invigorating touch of cold exposure.

Each technique is more than just a health hack; it's a loving invitation to reconnect with yourself, regulate your nervous system, and unlock a deeper sense of well-being—naturally, joyfully, and sustainably.

BREATHING YOUR WAY TO BETTER VAGAL TONE

Picture yourself standing at the edge of a serene lake, the surface so smooth it mirrors the sky. Your breath naturally syncs with the gentle lapping of the water, and for a moment, you feel deeply, effortlessly calm.

Good news: you don't have to move to a lakeside retreat to access that state. You can *breathe* your way there—anytime, anywhere.

Breathing isn't just a biological necessity; it's a secret weapon. By intentionally engaging your breath, you can tap into the calming power of the Vagus, rebalancing your nervous system and transforming how you manage stress, anxiety, and even your overall health.

In this chapter, we'll explore powerful breathing techniques designed to stimulate the Vagus and elevate your vitality in the process.

Diaphragmatic Breathing:

Activate Your Inner Calm

Think of your diaphragm—the broad muscle under your lungs—as your built-in massage therapist for your Vagus. Diaphragmatic breathing, also known as belly breathing, is a direct line to vagal activation.

How to do it:

- Lie on your back with your knees bent.
- Place one hand on your chest and the other on your belly.
- Inhale deeply through your nose, feeling your belly rise (your chest should stay mostly still).
- Exhale slowly through pursed lips, feeling your belly fall.

When you breathe this way, you're calming your heart rate, lowering stress hormones, and enhancing oxygenation. It's like sending your nervous system a handwritten invitation to chill.

4-7-8 Breathing:

A Rhythm That Resets You

As part of normal physiology, with every breath, our heart rate increases, and with every breath out, it slows (yes, it's that finely tuned). So, by increasing the cumulative time spent exhaling compared to inhaling, we can slow and calm our heart rate. Take diaphragmatic breathing up a notch with the 4-7-8 technique:

- Fully inhale through your nose for **4** counts.
- Hold the breath for 7 counts.
- Exhale slowly through pursed lips for **8** counts.
- If you feel too out of breath or uncomfortable, adjust the timing to suit your own lung capacity. For example, hold for 5 counts and exhale for 7 counts, or whenever your lungs are empty of air. Just make sure that the exhale is longer than the inhale.

This technique helps balance your autonomic nervous system, melts away tension, and invites a deeper sense of calm. It's like pressing the 'reset' button for your brain and body.

Alternate Nostril Breathing (Nadi Shodhana):

Find Your Center

Feeling frazzled or mentally scattered? Alternate nostril breathing harmonizes the brain's two hemispheres, promoting emotional equilibrium and mental clarity.

How to do it:

- Sit comfortably.
- Close your right nostril with your thumb and inhale through your left nostril.
- Close both nostrils briefly.
- Release your right nostril and exhale.
- Repeat, alternating sides for several rounds.

This practice is the yogic equivalent of rebalancing your Wi-Fi router —suddenly, everything starts working better.

Straw Breath (Kaki Pranayama):

Sip Your Way to Serenity

Imagine exhaling gently through a straw—this is the essence of Straw Breath. It's simple but potent for vagal activation.

How to do it:

- Inhale deeply through your nose.
- Purse your lips as if you're blowing through a straw.
- Exhale slowly and evenly, extending the breath as long as it feels comfortable.

This technique slows down your exhale, activating the parasympathetic nervous system—the 'rest and digest' mode your body craves.

Resonance Frequency Breathing:

Tune Your Breath to Your Best Self

Everybody has a natural breathing rhythm where heart rate variability (HRV)—the golden metric for vagal tone—peaks. This sweet spot is known as your **resonance frequency**.

How to explore it:

- Breathe at a slow, steady rate—around 5 to 7 breaths per minute (much slower than usual).
- Notice when you feel most relaxed yet energized—that's your resonance.

Finding and practicing your ideal breathing rate boosts emotional resilience, eases anxiety, and upgrades your overall vitality.

Box Breathing:

Your Portable Calm-Down Kit

When life throws high-stakes stress your way, Box Breathing is your secret weapon.

How to do it:

- Inhale for **4** counts.
- Hold your breath for **4** counts.
- Exhale for **4** counts.
- Hold again for **4** counts.

This method stabilizes the heart rate, reduces cortisol levels, and brings laser-sharp focus, like building an internal storm shelter whenever you need it.

Reflection Section: Your Breathing Journey

Consider keeping a breath journal for a week.

After each practice, jot down:

- *How you feel emotionally and physically*
- *Any shifts in mood, energy, or stress*
- *Which techniques resonated most with you (and which ones felt a little awkward—it's all part of the learning!)*

Breathwork Success Stories

Over the years, I've witnessed just how powerful breathwork can be—often in surprisingly immediate and tangible ways. I've seen it transform moments of overwhelm into calm, and fear into clarity.

Take an 11-year-old girl who struggled with anxiety attacks. She learned box breathing, and with just a little practice, she could use it on her own to steady herself when anxious feelings arose. It became her anchor in moments that used to feel unmanageable.

Or the woman in her 60s who developed a fear of driving after a stressful experience on the road. Travel triggered a wave of panic—until she began practicing 4-7-8 breathing before getting behind the wheel. With each breath, her anxiety softened. Over time, she reclaimed her confidence and her independence.

And personally? When life starts coming at me faster than I'd like—when the to-do list is long, the house is noisy, and everything feels a little *too much*—my go-to reset is slow, deep straw breaths. I pause, exhale fully, and intentionally relax my shoulders. Just a few breaths help me shift out of stress mode so I can choose my next step from a place of clarity rather than chaos.

Breathwork offers more than just physical perks; it's a gateway to mental clarity, emotional healing, and a deeper connection to oneself. Through the simple art of conscious breathing, you nurture your whole being—one inhale, one exhale at a time.

MAKE SOME NOISE! HUMMING, SINGING, AND CHANTING TO AWAKEN YOUR INNER HARMONY

Have you ever noticed how humming a tune can lift your spirits almost instantly? There's real science behind that simple, joyful act. Vocalization, whether through humming, singing, or chanting, creates vibrations that naturally stimulate the Vagus. These gentle internal vibrations originate from your vocal cords and travel outward, providing a soothing massage to this vital nerve, which promotes calmness, balance, and resilience.

Through this vibrational stimulation, you activate the parasympathetic nervous system—the 'rest and restore' branch—essentially pressing a natural reset button for your mind and body.

Begin with Something Beautifully Simple.

Find a comfortable position. Take a deep, mindful breath, and as you exhale, hum gently, feeling the resonance in your throat, chest, and even your face. Focus on specific sounds like **"Om"**, known for its deep, grounding resonance. Let the vibrations fill you from within. Practice for a few minutes each day and feel your nervous system gradually shift toward balance and peace.

But the benefits don't stop there. Singing and chanting don't just soothe the Vagus—they also unleash a flood of **endorphins** (your body's natural mood boosters) and **oxytocin**, the 'bonding hormone,' fostering feelings of joy, connection, and love. It's no wonder we instinctively turn to music in times of sorrow, celebration, and healing.

Infuse Daily Life with Musical Medicine.

Hum while you're cooking, driving, or showering. Hum softly as you work. Every note you create becomes a tiny act of self-care.

And for even greater impact, share your voice with others. Group singing amplifies the healing effect, infusing emotional connection and social support into the experience.

Interactive Element: Singing Circle

Host a weekly singing circle with friends or family. Choose songs that uplift and inspire, and enjoy the shared vibration. Over time, notice how these joyful gatherings nourish your spirit and strengthen your relationships.

By embracing the simple act of making noise, you invite more vibrancy, joy, and emotional healing into your everyday life—one beautiful breath, one hum, one song at a time!

The Healing Power of Sound Therapy

Sound is not just something you hear—it's something you feel. Vibrations travel through your body, influencing your cells, your mind, and your nervous system at a deep, primal level. Sound therapy harnesses this vibrational energy to stimulate the Vagus and promote relaxation and healing.

Different types of sound therapy offer unique benefits:

- **Music therapy** utilizes melodies and harmonies carefully selected to evoke emotions, calm the mind, and support healing.
- **Binaural beats** work by playing two slightly different frequencies in each ear; your brain synchronizes the difference, creating calming brainwave patterns that reduce stress and enhance focus.
- **Tuning forks,** when gently applied to specific points on the body, produce pure tones that harmonize your energy and stimulate vagal activity.
- **Tibetan singing bowls** generate rich, resonant sounds that seem to permeate every cell, inducing deep relaxation and opening pathways to physical and emotional healing.

These tools are not just for meditative moments; they can be used anytime you feel the need for a nervous system tune-up. And kids love experimenting with sound, too!

A newer area in sound therapy is **ASMR**—Autonomous Sensory Meridian Response. ASMR triggers a soothing, tingling sensation through delicate sounds, such as whispering, tapping, or gentle rustling. These sensory responses are thought to stimulate the Vagus, creating waves of relaxation. Many people find ASMR videos or audio recordings quite calming, offering an easy way to reset a frazzled nervous system.

Simple ways to bring sound healing into your day:

- Play soft, soothing music in the background while you work or unwind.
- Begin your meditation practice with the resonant tone of a singing bowl.
- Listen to binaural beats or nature sounds as you drift off to sleep.
- Explore ASMR recordings to find what uniquely soothes your senses.

Science supports what ancient traditions have long known: sound heals. Studies show that sound therapy can significantly enhance vagal function, reduce stress markers, and promote emotional balance.

The beauty of sound healing lies in its simplicity, and it's nearly effortless to incorporate into the rhythm of your daily life.

Through the intentional use of sound—your own voice or external frequencies—you awaken the healing intelligence of your body and spirit, returning yourself to harmony, one vibration at a time.

THE ART OF GARGLING FOR HEALTH

Sometimes, even the smallest of actions can have a positive impact on our health. Gargling—often overlooked as a mundane hygiene task—has the surprising benefit of being a tool for stimulating the Vagus and nurturing holistic health.

When you gargle, the rhythmic contractions of your throat muscles create vibrations that travel along the Vagus's pathway. This gentle activation enhances the nerve's function, boosting communication between the brain and body. In addition, stimulating the Vagus through gargling can also support healthy digestion and strengthen the immune system.

Here's how to transform gargling into a nourishing practice:

- Add about ½ teaspoon of salt (any kind) to 6-8 ounces of water that has been warmed on the stovetop or in a microwave.
- Take a small sip of the warm saltwater, known for its natural antimicrobial properties.
- Tilt your head back slightly, letting the water reach the back of your throat.
- As you exhale gently, create a bubbling sound, ensuring active engagement of your throat muscles. Gargle like you mean it!
- Aim to gargle for 30 seconds to one minute (obviously not all in one exhale),

Integrate it seamlessly:

Pair gargling with brushing your teeth or preparing for bed. Repeat two to three times a day for maximum benefit; however, even once a day is worthwhile, given the minimal time investment.

The combination of warmth and salinity not only soothes the throat but also encourages a thriving oral microbiome, helping prevent irritation, infections, and seasonal colds. Regular gargling becomes a defense system for your immune health and a simple act of self-care.

A Story of Healing:

Consider one woman who struggled for years with frequent sore throats and minor infections. After adding daily gargling to her routine, she noticed fewer infections, reduced mouth and throat irritation, and overall better health. Gargling became more than a task—it became a comforting daily ritual, a gentle reminder that small, mindful practices can create waves (or bubbles!) of healing.

Laughter—the universal language of joy—is one of the most delightful, effortless ways to stimulate the Vagus and uplift your entire being. Every genuine laugh will trigger rhythmic contractions in your diaphragm and abdominal muscles, sending activating signals through the Vagus. In response, your body floods with serotonin, endorphins, and oxytocin—the biochemical symphony of relaxation, pleasure, and connection.

In that moment of spontaneous laughter, you're doing more than feeling good—you're actively massaging your nervous system, easing tension, dissolving stress, and building emotional resilience. The positive afterglow of laughter can linger for hours, boosting mood, calming anxiety, and strengthening your natural capacity for joy.

How to Invite More Laughter Into Your Life:

- Play silly games with children or loved ones.
- Watch a favorite comedy or discover new stand-up acts.
- Listen to funny podcasts or audiobooks during daily routines.
- Share jokes, funny memes, or uplifting videos with friends to spark joy throughout the day.
- Spend time with playful pets—their unfiltered actions are natural laughter magnets!

Laughter Therapy:

Even when life feels heavy, laughter therapy can provide relief. This practice involves initiating gentle, voluntary laughter through playful exercises until genuine laughter bubbles up. Research shows that even 'pretend' laughter offers all the same benefits—lower stress, improved mood, enhanced immune function—as spontaneous laughter.

If there's one person in our household who has mastered the art of laughter, it's my daughter. From the time she was a baby, her laugh has been contagious—truly one of those bright, bubbling sounds that make it impossible not to smile. What amazes me is how intuitively she's learned to use it.

Sometimes, if she's feeling sad or upset, she'll start laughing—just like that—as a way to shift her mood. No one taught her this; it's something she figured out all on her own.

And of course, when she laughs, the people around her can't help but join in. Her laugh is just that joyful. It creates a positive feedback loop: she feels better, we feel better, and suddenly the mood in the room lifts.

Her brother gets it, too. If he sees her down, he'll swoop in with his best goofy older-brother antics—making silly faces, cracking absurd jokes, or breaking into wild dance moves—all with the mission of getting her to laugh. And it usually works. Sometimes, the two of them dissolve into uncontrollable giggles, laughing so hard they forget why they even started. Honestly, it's one of my favorite things to witness. It reminds me that laughter truly is medicine—free, spontaneous, and deeply healing.

I love my goofy kids. And I love that they've taught me (and reminded me) that joy doesn't always have to be sought—it can be created, any time, in the simplest and most beautiful of ways.

Laughter Strengthens Connections:

Laughter isn't just good for you—it's also good for your relationships. Sharing a laugh builds trust, dissolves barriers, and creates lasting emotional bonds. Group laughter is contagious, magnifying the healing effect exponentially. Whether you're sharing a funny story or giggling over life's absurdities, these shared moments nurture connection and a sense of belonging.

The next time life feels overwhelming, seek out a reason—any reason—to laugh. Let your body and spirit remember: joy is medicine. Laughter is a sacred, built-in healing technology, always available to elevate your vagal tone and brighten your life from the inside out.

Picture stepping into a cool shower at the end of a long, exhausting day. The crisp rush of cold water against your skin sends a wave of energy through your entire being, awakening your senses and grounding you firmly in the present moment. But this refreshing shock does more than invigorate – you guessed it, cold activates the Vagus!

As the body adjusts to the cold, the vagal pathways become engaged, promoting deep restoration, reducing inflammation, and enhancing physical and emotional resilience. Even the natural shivering response isn't random; it's part of your body's built-in mechanism to activate endorphins and norepinephrine—neurochemicals that lift mood, sharpen focus, and boost mental well-being.

Simple Ways to Invite Cold Therapy Into Your Life:

- **Cold Showers:** After a warm shower, gradually turn the water to cold for the final 30 seconds to a minute. Over time, you can extend this period as your tolerance builds.

- **Contrast Therapy:** Alternate between a sauna or hot bath and a cold rinse to enhance circulation and maximize benefits. For an invigorating finish, always end on cold.

- **Ice Water Facial Plunge:** Dip your face into a bowl of ice water for 10–20 seconds or splash cold water generously over your face. This instantly stimulates the Vagus through the dive reflex, bringing calm to the nervous system.

- **Carotid Massage with Ice:** Gently place an ice pack along the sides of your neck where the carotid arteries run. Best done lying down, and for no more than 1 minute on each side. This cool stimulation encourages vagal activation.

Brave the Chill: Cold Plunge Therapy for Vagal and Full-Body Health

If you've ever spotted a small, unassuming pool lurking near the sauna at your gym and wondered, *Who in their right mind would get in that?*— welcome to the world of cold plunge therapy. These icy little pools are typically kept between 40°F and 59°F, and yes, they feel *exactly* as cold as they sound.

But before you write them off as pure masochism, let's talk benefits— because this chilly dip might be just the reset your nervous system didn't know it needed.

Why (on Earth) Try It?

- **Vasoconstriction Superpowers**

  When you submerge in cold water, your blood vessels tighten to preserve heat. This constriction helps reduce inflammation and swelling in overworked or achy muscles and joints.

- **Better Circulation, Baby**

  As you rewarm, those same vessels reopen (vasodilation), flooding tissues with fresh, oxygen-rich blood. The result? Faster recovery and a delightful inner glow that isn't just from the hot tea you'll want afterward.

- **Mood-Boosting Endorphins**

  Cold exposure kicks your brain into gear, triggering a flood of endorphins. You'll often step out of the plunge feeling more alive, alert, and just plain *happier.*

- **A Kick in the Metabolism**

To keep you warm, your body kicks into high metabolic gear. That extra effort boosts calorie burn and gets your internal engine humming.

A Cold Plunge Success Story: My Husband, the Ice Warrior

My husband—bless his bold, adventurous soul—has turned the gym's cold pool into his personal ritual. Every workout starts with three whole minutes submerged in that frosty abyss. While he's in there, he practices extended box breathing to calm his mind and lower his heart rate.

The result? He emerges recharged. Even on days when he arrives at the gym tired or sluggish, the cold plunge flips the switch—he's able to run faster, lift heavier, and push through his workouts with more energy. He swears his recovery time is also quicker, with less soreness and improved joint mobility. I'll admit, I'm tempted... but still hovering near the edge!

Want Something a Bit More Targeted?

If the idea of a full-body icy dip feels like too much (totally valid), cryotherapy might be a gentler entry point. Many wellness centers now offer this modern take on cold therapy, using blasts of ultra-cold air for just a few minutes. Options range from whole-body chambers to localized treatments for specific sore spots. It's quick, high-tech, and surprisingly energizing—kind of like stepping into a cloud made of snowflakes and science.

A Quick Word on Safety

While cold therapy offers impressive benefits, it's not for everyone, and caution is key. Here's how to stay safe and smart:

- **Check with your doc** if you have cardiovascular or respiratory conditions, or if you're unsure whether cold exposure is right for you.

- **Start slow.** Try brief exposures and gradually increase the time and intensity.
- **Listen to your body.** Mild shivering is normal, but if you feel panicked, numb, or overwhelmed, get out and warm up.
- **Stay hydrated.** Cold immersion can be dehydrating. Sip some water before and after.
- **Warm up gradually** post-plunge. Wrap up in a towel, sip tea, or take a warm shower to help your body return to baseline.

Cold therapy might sound intense, but the rewards can be worth the temporary discomfort. It's one more tool in your wellness toolkit—a way to build resilience, reduce inflammation, and maybe even spark a bit of joyful aliveness in your day. Just remember to breathe... and maybe pack an extra towel.

Reflection Section: Self-Check-In

- *Which of these practices feels most natural to you?*
- *How might you add one or two of them into your daily or weekly rhythms?*
- *In what small ways have you already noticed shifts in your sense of well-being?*

Take a moment to honor your efforts so far. Each mindful breath, each nurturing choice, is a step towards a more vibrant, resilient you. Next, let's turn to one of the most vital and rejuvenating aspects of healing—restorative sleep.

Because healing doesn't just happen when we're actively doing; it also happens when we allow ourselves to simply 'be.'

4

VAGUS NERVE HACKS FOR SLEEP AND RELAXATION

The stillness of night isn't just a convenient time for Netflix marathons or scrolling through tomorrow's worries. It's when your body's most crucial work gets done — a silent masterpiece of healing, repair, and renewal quietly unfolding under the radar. Sleep isn't merely a passive state; it's the foundation of physical, mental, and emotional health. Yet, in today's world — where stress runs high and screen time stretches long — quality sleep often feels like chasing a moving target.

In my work as a healthcare practitioner, I've seen firsthand that when sleep improves, *everything* improves. And one of the key backstage players in this nightly production? You guessed it — the Vagus.

Our favorite nerve plays a surprisingly important role in regulating sleep-wake cycles by influencing the production of melatonin, the body's natural 'lights-out' hormone. Melatonin levels rise in response to darkness and help cue the body to wind down. The Vagus, through its intimate connection to the brain and the gut (where a large portion of melatonin is produced), helps keep this process humming along in sync with natural circadian rhythms. It's a delicate balancing act, and when the Vagus is supported, your internal clock tends to tick along more smoothly, helping you slide into sleep without a nightly battle.

When your vagal tone is strong and healthy, sleep often feels like slipping into a warm, cozy river that carries you effortlessly into morning. When it's weak? You may find yourself wrestling with the blankets at 2 a.m., solving imaginary problems, or pondering every awkward thing you said in middle school.

TECHNIQUES TO SUPPORT THE VAGUS FOR BETTER SLEEP

Research continues to pile up in favor of non-invasive Vagus stimulation for improving sleep quality. Clinical trials show that participants who stimulate their Vagus regularly experience more extended periods of deep sleep and fewer nighttime awakenings. Technology even offers gadgets designed to gently stimulate the Vagus — though many simple, at-home practices work wonders without any extra equipment.

So how can you actively support your Vagus to invite better sleep into your life? Here are some simple and effective techniques — no magic potions required.

Evening Breathing Exercises:

Simple, slow, diaphragmatic breathing is one of the most direct ways to engage the Vagus (see the previous chapter for 'how to'). Repeat for a few minutes before bed to signal to your nervous system: *The day is done. You may power down now.*

Neck and Shoulder Massages:

We often wear our stress like a pair of too-tight shoulder pads. Gently massaging the neck and shoulder areas can relax muscles along the Vagus pathways, easing you into a state where sleep comes more naturally. Slow, circular motions are best. Think of it less as giving yourself a massage and more like persuading your body to take off its metaphorical armor.

Another vagus-friendly technique worth an honorable mention: **Progressive Muscle Relaxation (PMR).** PMR is the practice of tensing and then releasing different muscle groups one by one, teaching your body (and brain) the forgotten art of letting go. It's like untangling a knotted-up necklace: one knot at a time, with patience and care.

Here's how to do it:

- Find a cozy, interruption-free spot (pets and toddlers permitting).
- Starting at your toes, clench them tightly for about five seconds, then relax completely. Feel the difference between tension and ease.
- Work your way slowly upward — calves, thighs, abdomen, chest, arms, shoulders, and even your forehead (where the 'thinking wrinkles' tend to live rent-free).
- As you relax each group of muscles, imagine tension draining away like water down a stream.

This gentle practice doesn't just *feel* good; it flips your parasympathetic nervous system into high gear. Studies have shown PMR can lower blood pressure, slow the heart rate, ease anxiety, and promote deeper, more restful sleep. In fact, some people find that PMR is so effective, they can barely finish the whole sequence before nodding off like a well-loved cat in a sunbeam.

Pro tip: If your mind tends to wander off during PMR (into lists, worries, or imaginary arguments), try using a guided audio recording to gently steer your focus back to your body.

SLEEP HYGIENE PRACTICES FOR OPTIMAL VAGAL FUNCTION

Sleep hygiene sounds clinical, but really, it's about making bedtime *inviting* again — the adult version of a lullaby and a storybook. Good sleep hygiene not only strengthens vagal tone but also supports all the systems that help you wake up feeling like a human instead of a zombie.

Here's where to start:

Consistent Sleep Schedules:

Going to bed and waking up at roughly the same time every day helps anchor your circadian rhythms. Yes, even on weekends. (I know. I'm sorry.) Think of it as setting your internal GPS for deep, restorative sleep.

Reduce Screen Time:

Screens (and the blue light they emit) are crafty little sleep thieves. If you must check your phone at night, consider blue-light-blocking glasses or installing apps that dim the screen's blue hues. Or better yet, pick up an old-fashioned book. Your Vagus (and probably your eyeballs) will thank you.

Create a Sleep-Friendly Environment:

- Cool, dark, and quiet rooms are ideal.
- Blackout curtains or an eye mask can work wonders.
- White noise machines, soothing playlists, or earplugs help muffle the random noises that seem ten times louder when we're trying to snooze.

Mind Your Meals and Drinks

Heavy meals, caffeine, and alcohol before bed are enemies of good sleep and happy vagal function. While it can be tempting to indulge late in the evening—especially after a long day—these dietary missteps can wreak havoc on your nervous system's ability to wind down.

Late-Night or Heavy Meals

Eating a large or rich meal close to bedtime forces your digestive system into high gear at a time when it should be slowing down. This delays the natural drop in core body temperature that signals your body it's time to sleep. It also diverts energy toward digestion instead of repair and restoration, which are the primary tasks of deep sleep. For some, this may also increase the likelihood of acid reflux or disrupted breathing patterns—neither of which is kind to restful sleep or vagal tone.

Sleep-Friendly Snacks

Late-night hunger pangs? Skip the chips and try these gentle, vagus-friendly options that support sleep rather than sabotage it. Tryptophan is an amino acid present in many high-protein foods. The body converts it into 5-Hydroxytryptophan (5-HTP), which then turns into serotonin, which then converts to melatonin. Our bodies are doing cool magic tricks like this with our food all the time! Here are a few ideas for smart bites to nudge you toward dreamland:

- **Banana + Almond Butter** - *Rich in magnesium, potassium, and tryptophan—this combo helps relax muscles and support melatonin production.*
- **Tart Cherry Juice (1/2 cup)** - *One of the few natural sources of melatonin. Sip an hour before bed to gently cue your circadian clock.*

- **Warm Oatmeal with Walnuts** - *Carbs help tryptophan reach the brain, while walnuts provide melatonin and healthy fats to keep you satiated.*
- **Chamomile + Honey** - *A classic! Chamomile calms the nervous system, while a drizzle of raw honey may help fuel your brain through the night.*

Caffeine: The Adenosine Antagonist

Caffeine works by blocking **adenosine**, a sleep-promoting neuro-transmitter that gradually accumulates in the brain throughout the day to build what's known as *sleep pressure*. When caffeine swoops in and hijacks those adenosine receptors, you may feel alert and energized. However, it also prevents you from naturally feeling sleepy when bedtime rolls around.

To make matters more challenging, caffeine has an average **half-life of about 5 hours**, meaning that even that innocent afternoon latte could still be stimulating your nervous system well into the evening. For sensitive individuals, even earlier caffeine consumption can subtly impair sleep depth and quality.

After receiving my SVT diagnosis, my cardiologist reminded me to cut back on caffeine. It made perfect sense—caffeine is an adenosine antagonist, and adenosine plays a key role in maintaining a steady heart rhythm. In fact, IV adenosine can be used in hospitals as a treatment for SVT, rapidly slowing and normalizing a racing heart.

And so, after more than two decades together, my long-standing relationship with coffee came to a bittersweet end. Goodbye, old bitter friend.

Caffeine Curfew – How to Outwit Your Inner Night Owl

Caffeine is a crafty stimulant—it sneaks into more than just coffee and sticks around long after that afternoon pick-me-up. Here's how to outsmart it:

Set a Cut-Off Time

For most people, caffeine after 12 p.m. is a gamble. Sensitive to it? Try cutting off by 10 a.m., or skipping it altogether and opting for herbal caffeine-free options like:

- Roasted dandelion root tea, Teeccino, or Cafix (roasted barley, rye, chicory, sugar beets)...Yes, I can vouch that these have a yummy coffee-like flavor!

Other Caffeine Sources to Watch for include:

- Green and black teas
- Pre-workout drinks and energy drinks
- Chocolate (especially dark varieties)
- Energy bars and protein powders
- Soda (even the "healthy" alternatives like Zevia)
- Some pain relievers and cold medications

Alcohol: The Sneaky Sleep Saboteur

Alcohol may feel like it helps you relax and fall asleep faster, but its effects on sleep architecture and vagal function are deceptive. As the body metabolizes alcohol, blood sugar levels may spike and then crash during the night, often resulting in middle-of-the-night wake-ups, restlessness, or vivid dreams. Additionally, alcohol suppresses REM sleep and interferes with the body's ability to regulate temperature and heart rate—key elements governed by the Vagus.

So what should you reach for instead? Sip that cup of warm herbal tea, or nibble a handful of those magnesium-rich almonds. Then, lean back, listen to your calming nighttime playlist, and marvel at how gloriously grown-up your choices have become.

NATURAL SLEEP BOOSTERS

Top 5 Supplements to Enhance Deep Sleep (Without Medication)

These gentle, research-backed supplements support your body's natural sleep cycles—no grogginess, no habit-forming chemistry. As always, consult your healthcare provider before adding anything new to your routine.

1. Magnesium (Glycinate or Threonate)

Calms the nervous system by boosting the production of calming neurotransmitters, relaxes muscles, and supports melatonin production. Best taken 1–2 hours before bed.

Magnesium threonate may also support brain function.

2. L-Theanine

A soothing amino acid found in green tea that promotes alpha brain waves—aka the 'pre-sleep chill zone.'

Great for easing mental chatter.

Pairs well with magnesium or melatonin.

3. Melatonin (Low Dose, 0.3–1 mg)

A natural hormone that helps regulate circadian rhythms.

Helpful short-term for jet lag, shift work, or disrupted sleep cycles.

More isn't better—high doses can backfire.

4. GABA (Gamma-Aminobutyric Acid)

An inhibitory neurotransmitter that tells your brain, "Hey, it's time to power down."

Especially helpful if stress or anxiety are keeping you up.

5. Glycine

A humble amino acid that lowers core body temperature and enhances sleep quality.

Found naturally in collagen-rich foods like bone broth.

Supplemental glycine before bed can deepen sleep and shorten sleep onset.

Incorporate Relaxation Rituals:

A warm bath, light stretching, mindfulness meditation, or aromatherapy (think lavender or chamomile essential oils) can all gently usher you toward sleep. You're essentially bribing your brain with pleasant experiences, and it works!

A Sleep Success Story: Reclaiming Rest Without a Single Pill

One story that continues to stick with me is that of a patient in his 40s —a veteran who had spent years working the night shift. By the time he came to see me, it had been a while since he'd left that schedule behind, but his body hadn't gotten the memo. His main complaint? Insomnia. He couldn't fall asleep until well past midnight, no matter how tired he felt.

He had what I lovingly call a "Yes, Doc" mindset—the kind of person who follows instructions to a T once he understands the logic behind them. So, when I explained how his circadian rhythm was essentially stuck in an old loop—and how specific lifestyle changes could help reset it—he dove in headfirst.

At the time, he had fallen into a cycle many people can relate to: staying up late watching TV because he wasn't tired, sleeping in to catch up, starting his day with a flood of caffeine, and saving any movement or exercise for later in the day when his energy finally picked up. Rinse and repeat.

But after our conversation, everything shifted. Even after a rough night's sleep, he made himself get up early and step outside first thing to soak in natural sunlight, helping boost his morning cortisol and quiet lingering melatonin. He skipped naps. He reduced caffeine. He moved his workouts to the morning. He shut off screens two hours before bed and even taped over all the tiny LED lights in his room— smoke detector, chargers, and all—to create true, pitch-black sleeping conditions.

Within just two months, this same man was falling asleep at his desired bedtime, waking up refreshed, and reporting that he felt better than he had in years. And here's the kicker: he didn't take a single supplement or sleep aid. Honestly, even I was a little surprised by how fast his results came. But his experience is a powerful reminder of the body's innate ability to recalibrate, especially when we create an environment that supports its natural rhythms.

That said, not everyone's sleep transformation is quite so straightforward. Over the years, many of my patients have needed a little extra support, whether in the form of calming botanicals, adaptogens, or gentle sleep-promoting supplements. This is especially true when someone's stress load is high or their work schedule doesn't allow for an ideal sleep schedule. In those cases, the right tools can act like a life raft, keeping the nervous system afloat until life circumstances can shift from the stress storm to calmer skies.

The truth is, there's no one-size-fits-all sleep formula. Your ideal routine might look different than someone else's. Your needs may change with the seasons of your life. And that's okay. Your body's path to rest is unique, and it deserves patience, compassion, and a willingness to experiment until you find what works.

The beautiful part? That path is absolutely within reach.

Reflection Section: Start a Sleep Journal

Want to get nerdy about your sleep (in the best way)? Try keeping a sleep journal for two weeks. Track your bedtime habits, which Vagus supporting techniques you use, and how you feel when you wake up. Over time, patterns emerge, and you'll gather invaluable insights about what's truly effective for you. Plus, it's strangely satisfying to have proof that your nightly breathing exercises are not just weird — they're working.

Bringing It All Together

Prioritizing good sleep hygiene and supporting your Vagus isn't just about clocking more hours under the covers — it's about transforming how you approach rest altogether. A strong vagal tone, nurtured by daily practices and mindful habits, helps ensure that sleep becomes a source of real healing rather than a nightly struggle.

While quality sleep sets the stage for healing, it's only one act in the grand performance of wellness. The next essential player? Movement. But don't worry—this isn't about breaking a sweat or chasing a personal best. We're talking about slow, nourishing movements that coax your Vagus—and your whole self—toward greater vitality. Let's step onto the mat and into the next chapter.

5

MOVEMENT TOWARD BETTER HEALTH: PHYSICAL EXERCISES FOR VAGUS VITALITY

W hen it comes to Vagus health, movement is medicine.

But not just any movement — we're talking about specific motions that massage, stimulate, and strengthen the body's parasympathetic 'calm-down' circuits.

THE POWER OF GENTLE YOGA

If you've ever stretched out on a yoga mat and thought, *"Ahhh, I could stay here forever,"* you're already onto something. Yoga isn't just about bending like a pretzel — it's an ancient practice that forges a sacred handshake between your mind and body.

Certain postures mechanically and energetically stimulate the Vagus by:

- Releasing tension along the spine (where the Vagus runs)
- Promoting diaphragmatic breathing
- Enhancing blood and lymphatic circulation
- Shifting the nervous system into 'rest-and-digest' mode

For those looking to give their Vagus some TLC, gentle restorative yoga is a beautiful place to start. These poses don't demand intense physical effort—just a little patience, a lot of kindness toward yourself, and maybe a cozy pair of sweatpants.

Supta Baddha Konasana (Reclining Bound Angle Pose)

This ultra-relaxing pose opens the pelvis and abdomen, boosting vagal signals from the gut upward.

How to do it:

- Lie on your back on a comfortable surface (mat, bed, carpet).
- Bring the soles of your feet together and let your knees fall open like butterfly wings.
- Support under each thigh with a pillow or block if needed for comfort.
- Rest your arms out to the sides, palms up.
- Close your eyes and breathe slowly, especially emphasizing a longer exhale.

Hold: 3–5 minutes.

Bonus Tip: Place a warm blanket over your belly for added vagal stimulation.

This posture enhances blood flow to the belly (hello, happy digestion!) while melting tension in the lower back. Mentally, it whispers, *"Let it all go,"* fostering a sense of surrender and acceptance. Emotionally, the gentle heart opening can lift spirits and spark soft feelings of compassion and love.

Viparita Karani (Legs-Up-the-Wall Pose)

This serene inversion is both restorative and invigorating. It facilitates blood and lymph return toward the heart and brain, which downshifts the nervous system.

How to do it:

- Sit sideways next to a wall, then gently swing your legs up as you lie back.
- Your hips can be flat on the floor or slightly elevated on a folded blanket.
- Rest arms out wide or on your belly.
- Relax your gaze or close your eyes.

Hold: 5–10 minutes.

Bonus Tip: Focus on feeling your heartbeat slowing down as you rest.

Perhaps the closest thing to an all-natural sedative. This pose resets circadian rhythms, soothes swollen feet, and presses a gentle pause button on a racing mind. Being upside-down (even just a little) shifts your perspective—literally and figuratively.

Setu Bandhasana (Bridge Pose)

Feeling a little sluggish? Bridge Pose to the rescue. It stimulates baroreceptors (blood pressure sensors), which talk directly to the Vagus.

How to do it:

- Lie on your back with knees bent, feet hip-width apart, close to your hips.
- Press into your feet and slowly lift your hips off the floor.
- Roll your shoulders under slightly and clasp your hands if comfortable.
- Keep the throat soft and the jaw relaxed.
- Breathe fully into the chest and belly.

Hold: 30 seconds to 1 minute, then slowly lower. Repeat 2–3 times.

Bonus Tip: As you hold this pose, feel into your sense of empowerment and stability. During Bridge pose, you may match your breath to your movement. Inhale to lift, exhale to soften slightly.

This movement stimulates the thyroid, enhances metabolism, and boosts energy levels. It opens the chest and shoulders, encouraging deeper breaths, which are basically the Vagus nerve's love language. Plus, it builds strength in the glutes and core while giving you that little victorious *"Hey, I did it!"* feeling.

Marjaryasana-Bitilasana (Cat-Cow Pose)

Here's your nervous system's version of a good morning stretch. This pose introduces a rhythmic flow that awakens the brain and the Vagus.

How to do it:

- Start on hands and knees, wrists under shoulders, knees under hips.
- Inhale: Arch your back, drop your belly, lifting both your tailbone and your gaze (Cow Pose).
- Exhale: Round your spine, press through your hands, tucking both your tailbone and chin to chest (Cat Pose).
- Repeat. Move slowly and match the movement to your breath.

Duration: 1–2 minutes.

This spinal flow gently massages your internal organs, promoting gut motility and easing digestive discomforts. The spinal flexion and extension enhance movement of spinal fluid, which can clear mental fog and improve focus, and create that luscious, *"Ah, my body is awake!"* feeling.

Parivarta Sukhasana (Seated Twist)

This easy seated twist releases physical and emotional stagnation and improves spinal flexibility. Compression and gentle twisting of abdominal organs trigger a parasympathetic rebound once released.

How to do it:

- Sit cross-legged or on a chair with feet flat.
- Inhale: Sit tall.
- Exhale: Twist gently to one side, placing one hand on the opposite knee and the other hand behind you.
- Keep the spine tall — imagine growing upward rather than cranking into the twist.
- Breathe into your belly.

Hold: 3–5 slow breaths per side.

Bonus Tip: With each inhale in a twist, imagine gathering light and energy. With each exhale, imagine releasing anything that no longer serves you.

Twists are nature's way of saying, *"Release the old; make space for the new."* A simple seated twist stimulates abdominal organs and detoxification processes. Energetically, this pose wrings out mental clutter, freeing up space for clarity and insight.

Balasana (Child's Pose)

The shape of this pose mimics the fetal position, offering a deeply primal sense of rest and protection.

How to do it:

- Kneel on the floor with your big toes touching and knees as wide as feels comfortable.
- Gently fold forward, letting your torso rest between your thighs.
- Extend your arms forward with palms down—or for a more restful version, let your arms drape alongside your body, palms up.

- Rest your forehead on the mat, a pillow, or your stacked hands.
- Breathe deeply into your back and belly.
- Hold: 1-5 minutes (or longer if it feels nurturing)

Bonus Tip: Imagine each exhale melting tension from your shoulders, spine, and jaw. Let gravity do the work. Try this mantra: Inhale and think, *"I invite ease."* Exhale and think, *"I release tension."*

This pose is like pressing a "reset" button for your whole being. Whether you're feeling overwhelmed, overstimulated, or just in need of a pause, Child's Pose is a safe harbor where your breath becomes the anchor.

A Real-Life Healing Moment: Child's Pose for Heart Rhythm Reset

In May 2025, a remarkable case report was published in Oxford Medical Case Reports that highlights just how powerful this gentle pose can be, not just for stress relief, but for real-time heart health.

A 27-year-old woman, who had been experiencing episodes of supraventricular tachycardia (SVT) since her teens, discovered she could consistently bring her heart back into a normal rhythm by entering Child's Pose. Unlike traditional maneuvers (like the modified Valsalva), which require assistance or a clinical setting, she was able to self-manage her episodes entirely on her own using this restorative position.

This simple, body-centered intervention not only empowered her but also opened the door for broader conversations about the role of yoga-informed practices in personalized cardiac care.

It's a gentle reminder that sometimes, the most potent medicine is the one that brings us closer to our own inner stillness.

Integrating yoga into daily life doesn't demand lengthy sessions or perfect poses. Start small: five minutes of stretching in the morning can set a peaceful tone for your day. Wind down with calming poses before bed. Technology offers many resources: explore apps, online classes, or even short video tutorials. Practicing yoga at home means no time wasted commuting or worrying about appearances. Yoga's greatest beauty is its accessibility: in comfy clothes, in your own space, at your own pace.

Through these gentle movements and moments of stillness combined, you build a sense of self-connection that nourishes both body and spirit.

Reflection Section: Keep a 'Yoga for Vagal Vitality' journal.

After each session, jot down:

- *How your body felt before and after*
- *Any emotional shifts*
- *Your favorite pose that day*

Over time, you'll uncover valuable patterns that deepen your practice and magnify its healing effects.

TARGETED STRETCHING: CLEARING THE VAGAL PATHWAYS

Muscles and fascia around the neck, shoulders, and spine are criss-crossed by vagus-adjacent structures. Tension here equals static on your internal communication lines.

Targeted stretches can free up these critical channels, improving signal clarity between brain and body.

Pro Tip: It's not the stretch itself — it's also how you breathe while stretching that truly activates the Vagus. Diaphragmatic breathing with long, slow exhales is the secret ingredient.

SCM (Sternocleidomastoid) Stretch

Releasing the SCM frees the Vagus where it runs near the carotid sheath; stretching this major neck muscle improves blood flow and eases mechanical pressure on the nerve. Additional benefits include sharpened mental focus, less anxiety, and easing headaches.

How to do it:

- Sit or stand tall.
- Tilt your head to the right (ear toward shoulder).
- Slightly turn your chin upward, as if looking at the ceiling.
- Feel a stretch along the side and front of your neck.
- Breathe deeply.

Hold: 30 seconds each side.

Tip: Go gently — no yanking.

Neck Rotations

Let's mobilize cervical structures near vagus pathways! Gentle neck movement softens guarding patterns in the upper trapezius and scalenes (which often pinch vagal pathways), and helps clear mental fog by increasing circulation to brainstem regions. Neck rotations may improve proprioception (body awareness) and enhance the quality of sleep.

How to do it:

- Slowly turn your head to the right.
- Pause and gently nod 'yes' a few times.
- Return to center.
- Repeat to the left.

Duration: 1 minute.

Tip: Add a chin-to-chest stretch and ear-to-shoulder tilts for a full-spectrum neck unwind. If your neck feels 'crunchy' or uncomfortable while nodding, just slowly rotate your head side to side like you're politely saying, "no thank you," at a buffet of stress.

Shoulder Rolls

Shoulder rolls might be the MVP of quick Vagus hacks, by releasing the thoracic outlet where nerves and vessels pass. This stretch opens the chest cavity, allowing for fuller diaphragmatic movement and improved breathing efficiency. It feels so good, like shrugging off emotional congestion.

How to do it:

- Lift your shoulders toward your ears.
- Roll them backward in a wide circle.
- Then roll them forward.
- Move slowly, feeling every micro-motion.

Duration: 5-10 circles in each direction.

EYE EXERCISES TO STIMULATE THE VAGUS

The eyes are windows to the soul—and hidden gateways to the Vagus. The cranial nerves controlling eye motion are direct cousins of the Vagus. Stimulating one often tunes the others.

Eye Circles

Gentle circular eye movements stimulate cranial nerve nuclei near the Vagus roots in the brainstem. This enhances ocular flexibility, eases headaches and tension, and improves resilience to stress.

How to do it:

- Without moving your head, slowly trace a large circle with your eyes clockwise.
- Then counter-clockwise.
- Move like you're tracing the rim of a giant slow-motion hula hoop.

Repetitions: 5 each direction.

Focus Shifting (Near-Far Gaze)

Focus shifting exercises the accommodation reflex, indirectly enhancing parasympathetic flexibility. This subtle movement improves mental adaptability, combats digital eye strain fatigue, and elevates mood.

How to do it:

- Hold your thumb about eight inches from your nose.
- Focus on your thumb, then shift focus to something far away, like a tree outside or an object across the room.
- Move back and forth slowly.

Repetitions: 5–10+ shifts.

Palming

This one feels so good if you're experiencing sensory overload. Warmth, darkness, and stillness bathe your optic nerve in serenity, easing both visual and emotional fatigue. Palming deepens relaxation, quiets mental chatter, and restores ocular lubrication (yes, even your eyeballs need downtime!).

How to do it:

- Rub your hands together briskly until warm.
- Gently cup your palms over your closed eyes without pressing.
- Relax your shoulders and breathe.

Duration: 1–2 minutes.

Screen breaks can boost your mood, focus, and energy. Set a timer to do 1-2 minutes of eye exercises every few hours. Your Vagus (and your screen-fatigued eyes) will thank you. You may even slow the progression of vision deterioration that can occur with age and excessive screen use!

Approach these movements intentionally, pausing whenever needed, layering them into your day.

As we move toward the next chapter, we'll shift our focus from movement to nourishment. What we feed our bodies directly influences how we feel, think, and thrive.

MAKE A DIFFERENCE WITH YOUR REVIEW

Unlock the Healing Power of Generosity

"The best way to find yourself is to lose yourself in the service of others."

— MAHATMA GANDHI

One of the most healing things we can do—both for ourselves and for the world—is to give freely without expecting anything in return.

If this book supported you on your path to greater health, resilience, or peace, would you consider taking one minute to help someone else begin that same journey?

My mission with *The Vagus Nerve Solution for Holistic Wellness* is to make stress relief, emotional balance, and natural healing simple and available for everyone. But to reach the people who need this information most, I am humbly requesting your help.

Most readers find books through reading reviews. Your review could be the encouragement someone needs to start reclaiming their well-being, especially if they're overwhelmed, burned out, or unsure where to begin.

Your few words could help…

- One more young adult to find relief from their anxiety.
- One more person with a chronic illness to feel empowered in their healing.
- One more overwhelmed mom to wake up feeling like herself again.

Simply go to the link below:

www.amazon.com/review/review-your-purchases/?asin=
B0FJQGF2X6

From the bottom of my heart, thank you. Your voice matters more than you know.

With gratitude,

Dr. Leia

6

EAT YOUR WAY TO A HEALTHY VAGUS: DIETARY AND HERBAL STRATEGIES

THE GUT-BRAIN AXIS: A NUTRITIONAL PERSPECTIVE

Imagine your gut and brain as two lifelong pen pals, constantly exchanging letters through a secret superhighway—aka the Vagus. This key player in your parasympathetic nervous system enables a back-and-forth dialogue that affects everything from digestion to mood. It's how neurotransmitters like serotonin and dopamine hitch a ride between your belly and your brain, influencing your emotional and cognitive state.

When this axis is in sync, you're more likely to feel clear-headed, emotionally grounded, and energized. But if something's off in the gut —like inflammation or an imbalanced microbiome—you might experience brain fog, anxiety, or even depression.

Support This Connection With:

- **Mindful Eating**: Slow down, savor each bite, and actually taste your food. Being present with your food aids digestion and signals safety to your nervous system.

- **Thorough Chewing:** We have molars for a reason (or at least that's what I tell my son when he's eating like a ravenous lion!). Reduce digestive drama by breaking food into easily digestible bits.
- **Screen-Free Meals:** Give your full attention to family, friends, and flavors, not emails or mediocre media.
- **Hydration**: Water is the VIP transport shuttle to get nutrients into our cells, and the sanitation crew to get waste out. Drink up throughout the day!
- **Meal Rhythms**: Regular mealtimes reinforce circadian rhythm and digestive flow. Bonus points for intermittent fasting—it gives your gut a break and enhances vagal tone.

Reflection Section: Mindful Eating Journal

Before and after meals, jot down your mood, energy level, and any tummy feedback. Over time, you'll spot patterns—and find your personal gut–brain harmony.

Anti-Inflammatory Foods for Vagus Vitality

Inflammation often starts quietly in the gut, then flares up everywhere—think of it as a slow-burning campfire that gets out of hand. When that happens, vagal tone takes a hit, and you might end up battling everything from joint pain to cardiovascular disease to anxiety.

Add These to Your Plate to Cool the Flames:

- **Omega-3s** from salmon, sardines, flaxseed, or walnuts. They soothe inflammation and boost nerve structure.
- **Antioxidant-rich berries**, like blueberries and pomegranates, help neutralize oxidative stress from free radicals (no, not the political type.) We're talking about unstable molecules that cause damage to DNA in cells and, gasp, aging!

- **Cruciferous veggies** like kale, broccoli, Brussels sprouts, and cabbage nourish gut health with juicy fiber and contain detox-supporting nutrients like sulforaphane (a powerhouse plant compound that may reduce the risk of cancer, diabetes, and heart disease)

Anti-Inflammatory Snack Idea

Mix a handful of walnuts with fresh berries and a sprinkle of cinnamon for a quick, vagus-loving pick-me-up.

Spice rack superheroes:

- **Turmeric:** contains the well-researched active compound, curcumin, which quenches inflammation in the brain, joints, gut, and more.
- **Ginger:** a gently warming root that stimulates digestion while calming inflammation.
- **Rosemary:** contains antioxidants and improves circulation and memory
- **Basil:** full of antioxidants that combat oxidative stress and chronic disease

*** Spice It Up! ***

Mix 1 tsp turmeric, ¼ tsp ground ginger, ½ tsp cinnamon, a pinch of black pepper, and warm coconut milk for an anti-inflammatory golden latte.

PROBIOTICS: TINY ALLIES FOR VAGUS HEALTH

Meet your **microbiome**—a bustling inner metropolis made up of trillions of microbes, many of which are more helpful than your average roommate. In fact, you're technically as much bacteria as you are human in terms of sheer cell count (yep, let that one sink in). These microscopic residents work hard to keep your digestive system running smoothly, bolster immunity, and even produce essential vitamins. But their influence doesn't stop at your gut—your Vagus is constantly eavesdropping on the microbial chatter, and what it hears can directly affect your mood, focus, and stress levels.

When your gut bacteria are happy, chances are you will be, too.

Strain Superstars

Not all probiotics are created equal—some strains go above and beyond for your mental and emotional well-being:

- **Lactobacillus rhamnosus**: This calm-inducing strain has been shown to reduce anxiety by influencing the nervous system. Think of it as a probiotic therapist for your gut.
- **Bifidobacterium longum**: This mood-boosting marvel supports the production of serotonin, your brain's happiness chemical. It's all about helping you feel more emotionally grounded and mentally resilient.
- **Lactobacillus helveticus**: A true stress-soother, this strain has been shown in studies to reduce cortisol levels and improve mood.
- **Lactobacillus plantarum**: Known for its ability to protect the gut lining and reduce inflammation, this multitasking strain may also enhance cognitive function and ease depressive symptoms.
- **Bifidobacterium breve**: This neuro-nurturing strain may support memory, learning, and brain plasticity—ideal for mental clarity and focus when life gets foggy.
- **Lactobacillus casei**: Found to have anti-anxiety and antidepressant effects, this strain helps modulate the gut-brain connection and supports emotional resilience during stressful times.

Research is revealing that the health benefits of probiotics are even more powerful when multiple beneficial strains are combined. It's a synergistic effect—like a wellness dream team. These helpful microbes actually work better when they're surrounded by their buddies, each bringing unique strengths to support your nervous system, immune health, and gut-brain harmony. The more, the merrier (and the healthier)!

In simple terms, when your gut flora is well-fed and diverse, your brain tends to function better, worry less, and cope more. Studies have found that specific strains can influence GABA, which helps calm the nervous system, proving that yes, a calmer gut really *can* mean a calmer mind.

Where to Find These Gut Goodies

Incorporating probiotics doesn't require a major lifestyle overhaul. In fact, it can be pretty tasty:

- **Fermented foods**: Add some sauerkraut to your salad, kimchi to your stir-fry, enjoy a glass of kombucha or kefir, or a dollop of yogurt. These are packed with natural probiotics that your gut will love.
- **Prebiotic-rich foods**: Beans, legumes, onions, garlic, and those ever-so-slightly underripe greenish bananas feed your good bacteria with resistant fiber. This fiber helps them produce short-chain fatty acids, which are like fuel for a thriving gut lining.
- **Supplements**: Prefer capsules to kraut? No problem. Choose a high-quality probiotic with multiple strains, proper storage (refrigerated or shelf-stable with proper packaging), and clearly labeled potency.

Microbiome Mood Boost Tip

Pair a probiotic-rich meal with a few minutes of deep breathing before eating to activate your Vagus and enhance digestion.

Bottom Line

Probiotics may be small, but their impact is mighty. They support your digestion, mental clarity, and Vagus health—all while asking for very little in return (just a little fiber and a decent home). By adding probiotic foods or supplements to your day, you're not just nurturing your gut—you're investing in a more balanced, energized, and emotionally balanced you.

FOOD AS NERVOUS SYSTEM NOURISHMENT

Let's talk about something that happens every day, multiple times a day: eating. But what if your meals could do more than satisfy hunger? What if they were actually a form of therapy—for your Vagus, no less?

Every bite you take sends signals through your body—tiny messages that either support your vagal tone or stress it out. Whole, unprocessed foods are the rockstars here. They're packed with the nutrients your body actually recognizes and knows how to use, without the extra burden of synthetic additives and preservatives.

Think of it this way: when you eat foods in their natural state—like fresh vegetables, fruits, whole grains, and lean proteins—you're feeding your cells exactly what they need to thrive. It's like giving your body a clear instruction manual rather than a confusing string of vague suggestions.

Fiber: Nature's Gentle Detox

Fiber might not be the most glamorous topic, but your gut absolutely loves it. It acts like a soft broom sweeping through your digestive tract, keeping things moving and feeding your healthy gut bacteria along the way.

Whole grains like quinoa and oats, along with fruits, veggies, beans, and legumes, should be regulars on your plate. Bonus points if you vary your fiber sources—it keeps your microbiome happy and diverse.

Balance Your Macronutrients

Here's a quick breakdown of what your body's asking for:

- **Carbohydrates** provide energy—your brain's favorite fuel.
- **Proteins** help repair tissues, support your immune system, and aid hormone production.
- **Healthy fats**—like those in avocados, nuts, seeds, and olive oil —are essential for nerve health and brain function. Think of them as the lubricant for your inner communication network.

So, the goal? A balanced plate. Not perfect, not Instagram-worthy— just real, colorful food that fuels your body and keeps your nervous system humming.

Don't Forget to Hydrate

Water might seem basic, but it's non-negotiable for vagal health. It helps with everything from nutrient transport to cellular repair to mental clarity. Aim to sip consistently throughout the day rather than gulping it all at once. And yes, herbal teas count! Especially tummy tonics like chamomile, peppermint, or ginger—they hydrate while also offering nervous system support.

Smart Habits for Stress-Free Eating

Success with anything, including creating a nourishing diet, is largely dependent on good planning. Meal planning might not sound exciting, but it's essential for staying on track. Set aside a little time each week to plan, prep, and shop with intention. That way, when hunger strikes or stress hits, you're not scrambling for the nearest bag of chips.

Meal planning became a survival skill for me, born out of necessity as a busy working mom. I knew I couldn't swing multiple grocery trips each week, so I created a simple system that has saved my sanity more times than I can count. On the side of my fridge lives a little magnetic whiteboard where I map out our weekly meals in a grid. The days of the week run down the left-hand side, and "breakfast," "lunch," and "dinner" stretch across the top. I fill in each square with what we'll eat, then use that plan to make the grocery list on the spot.

And because life has a way of throwing curveballs, I always plan for the unexpected. I keep a stash of healthier frozen meals and grab-and-go snacks on hand just in case the day gets derailed and I'm unable to cook what's on the menu. It's still a better (and more budget-friendly) option than defaulting to fast food. This little ritual of planning ahead has helped take the stress from feeding my family—and made it easier to stay on track with nourishing choices.

Also, get friendly with food labels. They're like mini detective cases— you just need to know what to look for. Avoid ingredients you can't pronounce, and aim for short, simple lists. You can get phone apps like Yuka to scan and analyze food labels so you can learn at a glance which products are a thumbs up and which ones you should avoid.

Avoiding Common Pitfalls

Let's face it—some habits are hard to break. Overeating, mindless snacking, and emotional eating often have less to do with willpower and more to do with unmet emotional needs. If you find yourself eating from stress, boredom, or habit, pause and ask: *What do I really need right now?*

Maybe it's a deep breath. Perhaps it's a walk around the block. Maybe it's a moment of stillness. If you feel like you're really struggling to break free of your bad habits, Holistic counseling can help you uncover the beliefs and patterns that keep you stuck—and gently guide you toward new ones that actually serve you. You can find out more at drleiaanderson.com.

Also, if you avoid certain foods for medical, ethical, or religious reasons, honor that. For instance, if you're vegan and missing out on omega-3s from fish, an algae-based supplement is a great option.

Keep It Consistent, Not Perfect

This isn't about perfection—it's about momentum. Real change comes from small, sustainable steps, not drastic overhauls. Pick one habit to start with—maybe drinking more water, adding a veggie to lunch, or planning two meals a week—and build from there.

Progress over perfection. Always.

Your relationship with food is a powerful foundation for vagal health. When you approach meals with intention and care, you're not just feeding your body—you're nourishing your nervous system, your emotional well-being, and your whole sense of vitality.

Coming up next: plants you may or may not find in the grocery store that offer support for your parasympathetic nervous system. Let's step into the garden together.

HERBAL ALLIES FOR VAGUS SUPPORT

Herbs have long been trusted companions on the path of natural healing. When it comes to Vagus support, they offer a gentle yet effective way to calm and restore the nervous system. One group of herbs that shines in this area is **nervines**—plants that nourish, soothe, and balance the nervous system. Some calm you down when you're frazzled, others help rebuild strength after burnout, and many do a little of both.

You can take nervines in the morning or afternoon to promote calm throughout the day, or in the evening to support restful sleep. Here are some key players to consider adding to your healing toolkit:

Nervines: Calm in a Cup

- **Milky Oat Seed** (Avena sativa): A true restorative, this trophorestorative herb helps rebuild and strengthen frazzled nerves. Think of it as a balm for burnout—soothing, replenishing, and grounding.

- **Chamomile** (Matricaria chamomilla): This classic calming herb does double duty. It relaxes both mind and body while reducing inflammation. Chamomile is an antispasmodic (eases muscle tension) and a vulnerary (heals irritated tissues like the gut lining). Safe for kids and lovely in tea.
- **Lemon Balm** (Melissa officinalis): Brightens the mood and eases digestive upset. It's uplifting without being overstimulating. Note: Lemon balm is mildly thyrosuppressive, so those with hypothyroidism should use caution.
- **Valerian Root** (Valeriana officinalis): A bedtime favorite for anxious minds and tight muscles. This warming herb supports deeper sleep, especially for those with a colder constitution.
- **Passionflower** (Passiflora incarnata): Great for racing thoughts and bedtime worry. This anxiolytic (anxiety-soothing) herb promotes calm without sedation.
- **Skullcap** (Scutellaria lateriflora): Ideal for tension held in the body, especially when stress hits the gut. This herb eases nervous digestion and supports motility.
- **Verbena or Vervain** (Verbena officinalis): Particularly helpful for those who push themselves to exhaustion. It balances the sympathetic and parasympathetic systems and is useful for burnout, insomnia, anxiety, or low mood.

Sip Tip

Try chamomile, lemon balm, and passionflower together in a calming tea blend before bed.

Adaptogens: Nature's Stress Shields

Another powerful class of herbs for Vagus support is **adaptogens**. These amazing plants help your body adapt to daily stress, balancing the autonomic nervous system and enhancing overall resilience.

Adaptogens don't just blunt the symptoms of stress—they help your body respond more efficiently and recover more quickly. Think of them as your behind-the-scenes support crew, strengthening your foundation from the inside out.

Top Adaptogenic Allies

- **Ashwagandha** (Withania somnifera): A calming adaptogen that helps lower cortisol levels (your primary stress hormone). It supports relaxation, sleep, and a sense of grounded calm. A staple of Ayurvedic medicine.
- **Rhodiola** (Rhodiola Rosea): Gently energizing, Rhodiola boosts mental clarity and stamina without the jitters of caffeine. Ideal for fatigue, low mood, or burnout.
- **Holy Basil or Tulsi** (Ocimum tenuiflorum): Revered in Ayurvedic tradition for restoring the nervous system after chronic stress. Tulsi helps reduce inflammation and stabilize blood sugar, promoting emotional resilience and mental clarity.
- **Maca or Peruvian Ginseng** (Lepidium meyenii): Native to the Andes, Maca root enhances stamina, libido, and endocrine function. It's an excellent choice for hormonal balance and overall vitality, especially during times of high demand.
- **Eleuthero or Siberian Ginseng** (Eleutherococcus senticosus): Known for boosting endurance, Eleuthero is a gentle yet effective adaptogen that enhances stamina, mental performance, and immune strength, especially under prolonged stress. It's particularly helpful for those recovering from illness, burnout, or chronic fatigue.
- **Cordyceps Mushroom**: A unique adaptogen that improves oxygen use and boosts energy at the cellular level. It's beneficial for physical endurance and immune resilience.
- **American Ginseng** (Panax quinquefolius): A powerful tonic that supports mental alertness, stamina, and immune function. Best for short-term use when you need a strong push, like during significant life transitions or intensive workloads.

These herbs don't stimulate or sedate—they normalize. Over time, they help regulate stress hormones, improve resilience, and enhance vagal tone without overwhelming the system.

Why Adaptogens Matter for Vagal Health

Chronic stress disrupts the balance of the autonomic nervous system, often tipping us into sympathetic overdrive (hello, fight or flight). Adaptogens help prevent that. They enhance your ability to stay balanced and grounded - even when those inevitable things we don't want to happen, happen, and life hits a rough patch.

Studies show that adaptogens support faster recovery from stress, reduce fatigue, and improve focus. The cumulative effect? Greater emotional stability, physical endurance, and long-term vitality.

Bitters & Carminatives: For the Gut-Vagus Connection

Since so much vagal activity originates in the gut, it's worth highlighting herbs that directly support digestive function. These herbs don't just help with bloating—they also improve vagal tone by encouraging healthy gut motility and calm.

Bitters are herbs with a sharp, often earthy taste that stimulates digestive secretions—like stomach acid, bile, and enzymes—by activating bitter taste receptors. This stimulation activates the Vagus and primes the digest part of the "rest and digest" response.

Carminatives are herbs that help prevent or relieve gas and bloating by calming and relaxing the muscles of the digestive tract and reducing inflammation.

Gut-Loving Herbal Helpers:

- **Cardamom** – A warming, aromatic carminative that blends beautifully into teas or meals. Supports digestion and eases heaviness or nausea.
- **Coriander Seeds** – Mild and sweet, coriander eases bloating and is especially helpful when digestion feels sluggish.

- **Peppermint** – Cools and calms the gut. Great for bloating and cramping, and especially helpful when digestive issues are tied to stress or anxiety.
- **Dandelion Root** – A classic bitter tonic that supports liver function and digestion. Remember those coffee alternatives? Dandelion root tea is a great one!
- **Fennel** – Lovely in tea or meals, fennel helps relieve gas and supports digestive comfort. It's gentle and effective—like a lullaby for your belly.
- **Gentian Root** – One of the most intensely bitter herbs out there. A little goes a long way in stimulating digestion and vagal tone.
- **Artichoke Leaf** – Another potent bitter that supports liver and gallbladder function, while also enhancing digestive flow.

How to Invite These Herbs into Your Life

You don't need to be an herbalist—or have a complete home apothecary—to benefit from plant medicine. Start simple:

- Brew herbal teas and enjoy them as part of your winding-down ritual.
- Try glycerites or tinctures for concentrated support—just a dropperful can make a difference.
- Add culinary herbs like cardamom, ginger, fennel, or basil to your meals regularly.

Smart Use = Safe Use

Herbs can be powerful medicine—but like all powerful tools, they should be used with care. Here's how to incorporate them wisely:

- **Start slow**: Begin with the lowest effective dose and increase gradually.

- **Pay attention**: Tune in to how your body responds. Herbal medicine is a conversation, not a command. If anything makes you feel overstimulated or oversedated, try reducing your dose or switching to a different herb.
- **Consult a pro**: Especially if you're on medications or have underlying health conditions, a certified herbalist or Naturopathic Doctor can help tailor herbs to your specific needs.
- **Choose quality**: Source your herbs from trusted brands that follow Good Manufacturing Practices (GMP), such as:
  - Gaia Herbs
  - Heron Botanicals
  - Wise Woman Herbals
  - Herb Pharm

Pro Tip

Look for organic, sustainably sourced ingredients. The vitality of the plant matters, just like yours.

Healing with the Help of Plants

Herbs are a daily part of my life. I take them regularly, share them with my family, and prescribe them to patients when the match is right. When used thoughtfully and with a clear purpose, plant medicine can be a true game-changer.

Here's just one example—if I shared all the positive experiences I've had with plant medicine, we'd need an entirely separate book! Earlier this year, after recovering from a viral illness, I found myself wiped out—low energy, sluggish motivation, just not feeling like myself. I turned to a blend of adaptogenic herbs: cordyceps, ashwagandha, rhodiola, Panax ginseng, and eleuthero. Within days, I began to feel my energy return, like a light gradually turning back on. These herbs didn't just mask my fatigue—they helped me to bounce back from the stress of the illness and restore vitality at a foundational level.

Over the years, I've seen herbal remedies support patients dealing with a wide range of challenges—from fibromyalgia and chronic fatigue to anxiety, IBS, and other conditions tied to Vagus nerve imbalance. These aren't isolated stories. This isn't just folk wisdom passed down through the ages. There's a growing body of scientific research validating how specific plant compounds interact with our biology to help the body function more efficiently, more calmly, and more resiliently.

In Summary

Herbs are not just remedies—they're relationships. Whether you're sipping calming nervine tea or adding adaptogens to your morning routine, you're inviting nature into your healing process.

By incorporating botanical medicine into your daily life, you're:

- Supporting your Vagus
- Enhancing stress resilience
- Promoting emotional balance and vitality

Plants can be powerful. And when used with care and intention, they can offer some of the most elegant, effective tools for nervous system support and whole-person healing. As we end this chapter, take a moment to reflect:

Which herbs are calling to you right now, and how might they support your journey?

7

CREATING A VAGUS-FRIENDLY ENVIRONMENT

HAPPY HOME, HAPPY VAGUS!

Transforming your home into a haven of calm isn't just about how it looks; it's an act of intentional care for your nervous system. Your surroundings impact how you feel, think, and function, especially when it comes to the Vagus. Every detail, from wall color to ambient sound, has a physiological effect. When your home supports peace, your body receives that message and responds with greater ease and calm.

When your environment feels safe, your nervous system begins to believe it, too.

The Hidden Noise of Modern Life

Let's start with sound—one of the most underestimated influences in the home. The steady hum of traffic, a blaring TV, or the buzz of appliances and electronics creates background stress that can surreptitiously keep your body in a state of alert. These sounds might seem small, but over time, they can contribute to mental fatigue and vagal overload.

Consider lowering the volume of your environment:

- Turn off electronics when not in use, and turn the Wi-Fi off at night.
- Use rugs, curtains, or sound-absorbing panels to soften echoes (I found acoustic panels that look like artwork to put in my cavernous stairwell!).

The Sound of Stillness

Nature sounds, soft instrumental music, or even silence itself can create a sense of sacredness in your space. Research shows that soothing soundscapes positively influence vagal activity and stress resilience.

Choose a few go-to soundtracks that support your mood:

- Ocean waves for grounding
- Forest rain or a crackling fireplace for gentle release
- Slow, ambient music for focused calm

Let your home be a symphony of peace, crafted with care.

Let There Be (Natural) Light

Light plays a key role in setting your biological circadian rhythms. Exposure to natural light during the day helps stimulate serotonin—the 'feel good' neurotransmitter—and supports melatonin production at night to aid restful sleep.

Try This:

- Arrange your favorite reading or work areas near a sunny window
- Open your curtains wide in the morning, as soon as possible after waking up
- Use full-spectrum lighting in darker rooms

Picture waking up to gentle sunlight filtering through gauzy curtains, slowly nudging you into the day. If you need to have blackout curtains due to city lights outside your bedroom window, use a sunrise alarm clock to ease into awakening. On cloudy days or if you wake up before sunrise, consider using a UV-free light therapy lamp with at least 10,000 lux brightness, such as the 'Happy Light.' Turn on the light for 10-15 minutes right after you wake up, for example, in the bathroom while you're getting ready for the day or in the kitchen while you're prepping coffee and breakfast. Many of my patients have reported that this simple hack of getting bright light first thing in the morning (whether it be the sun or a sun simulator) has helped their seasonal depression, daytime energy, and sleep quality.

Bringing Nature Indoors

Natural elements have a soothing effect on both the body and mind. Houseplants, in particular, have been shown to reduce stress and increase feelings of vitality. The act of caring for plants—watering, pruning, noticing new growth—encourages mindfulness and calmness.

If you're new to plant care, start simple. Snake plants, ZZ plants, and pothos are forgiving and flourish in many environments. Add a tabletop water fountain to infuse your space with the tranquil sounds of trickling water, like bringing a miniature stream into your home.

The Power of Color and Texture

Color and texture send direct signals to the brain. Cool, calming shades like soft blues, gentle greens, and warm neutrals evoke safety and serenity. They subtly mirror the calming forces of nature—clear skies, leafy forests, sun-warmed stones. Incorporate real wood and stone as much as you can in your home, furniture, and décor. I love decorating my home with naturally beautiful items such as seashells my kids collected at the beach, geodes, polished rocks placed on the soil in my houseplant pots, and glass or crystal suncatchers hung in the windows.

Incorporate cozy textures to activate the parasympathetic nervous system:

- A chunky knit throw for your reading chair
- A thick, plush rug underfoot
- A soft linen duvet on your bed

The body relaxes more easily when your senses feel comforted and anchored in warmth.

CLEARING SPACE, CLEARING STRESS

Visual clutter creates mental clutter. It sends a signal of chaos to the brain, keeping the mind on high alert. Creating a calm space doesn't have to mean embracing minimalism to the extreme, but it does mean surrounding yourself only with what you need, love, and use.

Decluttering Ritual:

- Choose one surface (a nightstand, coffee table, countertop, or desk)
- Clear it completely
- Add only what feels supportive, meaningful, or beautiful

Even a single tidy corner can become your sanctuary—a retreat for reading, meditation, or quiet thought. However, the more space that can be organized for calm in your home, the better! I remember years ago when I first picked up Marie Kondo's book 'The Life-Changing Magic of Tidying Up'. I began folding laundry using her method, creating compact rectangles of fabric that can be stored vertically in a drawer or on a shelf – it was actually satisfying to do laundry, visually appealing to look in my closet and drawers, and no more forgetting I had clothes that were forever of the bottom of a pile of pancake-stacked items. Indeed, sometimes a little tidying can be life-changing!

*** 3-Item Declutter Challenge ***

Pick a countertop, shelf, or drawer. Remove three items and put them away, donate, or recycle. Feel that mental weight lift?

Scents That Soothe

Scent is a potent mood regulator. Essential oils like lavender, bergamot, and chamomile activate brain regions involved in emotion and memory. These fragrances help signal safety to the body, calming the nervous system with each breath.

Try diffusing oils throughout your home or incorporating them into a bath or massage routine. Even one drop on a warm compress can shift the atmosphere around you—and within you.

Reflection Section: Sensory Exploration Exercise

Take a few quiet minutes in your space. Close your eyes and tune into your senses:

- *What sounds surround you?*
- *What scents drift through the air?*
- *How do the textures beneath your fingertips feel?*
- *What visual elements soften or distract your mind?*

This check-in invites you to recognize what supports you and what may need to shift. The more attuned you become to your environment, the more empowered you are to shape it in a way that nurtures you.

Your Nervous System's Sanctuary

A vagus-friendly home isn't about perfection—it's about intention. Think about how you want your home to *feel*, not just how you want your home to look. You're creating a space that supports rest, connection, and joy. When your environment reflects peace, your nervous system follows suit.

EMBRACING NATURE: OUTDOOR ACTIVITIES FOR VAGAL HEALTH

Let the Earth Heal You

There's something undeniably soothing that happens when we find ourselves fully enveloped by the natural world. Picture this: you're standing on the edge of a dense forest. The air is rich with the earthy scent of damp leaves, almost like a pungent, grounding perfume. Branches sway in the breeze, and you hear nothing but the gentle rustling of leaves and joyful chattering of birds. You feel yourself sigh, releasing the tension of modern life. You close your eyes and inhale deeply. In this moment, something within you softens.

This is a state of calm that's a deeper, almost spiritual opportunity for healing. Nature, in all its untouched splendor, holds an intrinsic power to restore and renew. It serves as an invisible balm for our overstimulated nerves, offering a vital boost to vagal tone, helping to calm the body's stress responses, and inviting us into a profound sense of peace.

Nature as a Nervous System Ally

Natural spaces offer refuge from the constant stimulation of modern life. In these green sanctuaries, our minds find the respite they crave. The soft hues of greens and browns relax the eyes. Crisp, clean air fills the lungs. This immersion in nature automatically initiates a parasympathetic response—lowering cortisol levels, reducing blood pressure, and promoting feelings of safety and belonging.

Nature reminds us that we're part of something larger—a quiet belonging that calms the soul.

Studies show that regular time spent in forests, near water, or in green spaces significantly improves mental health, lowering anxiety and depression, while lifting mood and cognitive function. Even brief moments beside a gentle stream or beneath a canopy of trees offer a kind of restoration that transcends logic—it's felt in the body and spirit alike.

Forest Bathing: An Immersion in Calm

One beautiful practice that embodies this connection is *forest bathing*, or **Shinrin-Yoku**. Rooted in Japanese tradition, forest bathing invites us to fully engage with nature through all five senses.

To begin, find a peaceful natural setting. Think about places like a local park, a national park, a botanical garden, or your own property. Stroll. Let each step land gently. Tune in deeply:

- Listen to the rustle of leaves
- Watch light dance through branches
- Touch the rough bark of a tree
- Smell the scent of pine or damp soil
- Feel the breeze kiss your cheeks

As you walk, you're not trying to reach a destination—it's about achieving a state of presence. Let your thoughts fall away. Let the forest speak in its quiet language. Forest bathing is less about doing and more about being, allowing your nervous system to sink into a state of effortless calm.

Hiking: Rhythmic Movement, Rhythmic Breath

Hiking combines the benefits of exercise, rhythmic movement, and outdoor immersion—all of which enhance vagal tone. Whether you're meandering through a meadow or trekking up a wooded hill, hiking encourages you to sync your breath with your steps. This natural rhythm soothes the nervous system and fosters mindful awareness.

Feel your muscles respond to the terrain. Notice how your lungs expand. Tune into the heartbeat of the land beneath your feet. Each trail walked is a meditation in motion—an embodied reminder that you're capable, connected, and very much alive.

Gardening: Growing Calm from the Ground Up

There's something deeply satisfying about tending to a garden. Digging into rich soil, planting seeds, watching them sprout into life— it's a ritual of patience, observation, and care.

Gardening provides a sensory-rich experience:

- The texture of the soil in your hands
- The scent of herbs and flowers
- The simple joy of watching growth unfold

This act of nurturing mirrors our own inner healing process; it slows us down and anchors us in the present moment. It connects us to the rhythms of life and death, bloom and decay, rest and rebirth. The Vagus thrives in this kind of mindful engagement.

Grounding: Barefoot Connection to the Earth

Grounding—also known as earthing—is the practice of placing your bare feet directly on natural surfaces like grass, soil, or sand. Simple as it sounds, this tactile connection with the Earth can have a calming, restorative effect on the nervous system.

How to Practice Grounding:

1. Find a safe, natural space free of sharp debris
2. Remove your shoes and socks
3. Stand or walk slowly, focusing on the sensations
4. Breathe deeply and allow tension to release

Feel the cool morning dew, the sun-warmed sand, or the tickle of blades of grass. This direct contact connects you to Earth's stabilizing energy, helping to discharge stress and support emotional balance. Many people who practice grounding regularly report feeling calmer, more centered, and more attuned to their environment. I know that if I go too long without touching nature, I begin to crave it!

Let Nature Rewire You

Outdoor activities like forest bathing, hiking, gardening, and grounding are far more than hobbies or diversions—they are rituals of nervous system repair. They call us back to our senses. Back to our breath. Back to the Earth.

These moments in nature don't just help us cope—they help us remember who we are.

By inviting these simple practices into your regular routine—even once a week—you create space for your vagal health to thrive.

Coming Up Next...

In the next chapter, we'll explore the inner landscapes of the mind and heart. Through mindfulness, meditation, and mindset shifts, you'll learn how to further strengthen your vagal tone from within.

But for now, step outside. Take a breath. Let the sky expand above you and the ground hold you steady. Let nature do what it does best—heal, quietly and completely.

8

THREE M'S FOR VAGUS MASTERY: MINDFULNESS, MEDITATION, AND MINDSET

MINDFULNESS PRACTICES FOR STRESS RESILIENCE

Picture yourself standing by the ocean, feeling the gentle waves lapping at your feet. You focus on the sensation of water receding beneath your toes. This simple act of being present captures the essence of **mindfulness**—a state of awareness without judgment. It's about acknowledging each moment as it unfolds.

Mindfulness isn't just a buzzword; it reshapes how we interact with the world, including our own bodies. Fostering present-moment awareness enhances calmness, emotional regulation, and vagal tone. As you become more attuned to your body's signals, stress and anxiety naturally diminish, leaving space for clarity.

Core principles like non-judgmental observation and self-awareness serve as the cornerstones of mindfulness. They encourage you to observe your thoughts and emotions without assigning value or becoming swept away by them. This practice cultivates emotional resilience, reduces stress, and enhances overall well-being.

The mind-body connection is truly mind-blowing. Positive emotions generated through mindfulness—like joy, compassion, and gratitude —ripple through your body, soothing the nervous system and strengthening vagal tone.

Our tendency to dwell on past regrets or future anxieties often fuels chronic stress. The past, while influential, cannot be altered. The future remains elusive—a vast landscape of infinite possibilities that can overwhelm. Anxiety stems from the illusion that we can control what hasn't happened, while depression often arises from the belief that change is impossible.

In contrast, the present moment is real and manageable. Life unfolds in the now. When overwhelmed, try asking yourself:

"Am I okay right now?"

I know... "okay" is a somewhat subjective term. Maybe a tiger isn't actively chasing you, but you are not where you want to be in life financially. Or you're in physical pain. Or you're in emotional anguish. And maybe you're not actually "okay" with feeling those things because you wish things were different.

The idea here is to acknowledge that if you are not in an acute life-or-death situation, you are, in fact, okay. By tuning into the reality of the moment and acknowledging your okay-ness, you put life in perspective, take off some pressure, and allow the nervous system to relax. Acceptance doesn't mean lying to yourself that everything is fantastic if it's not. And it doesn't mean that you stop moving toward improvement.

In fact, if we greet each moment with compassion, acceptance, curiosity, and openness, it helps us to be in a calm state, which enables us to remain clear-headed, problem solve, and make better decisions (which leads to life improvements!).

This simple check-in – "Am I okay right now?" – can help you anchor to the present moment—the only place where life truly happens.

One of the most effective anchors to the present is your breath. It's always with you, always available. Breath awareness techniques—such as observing your natural breath or counting breaths—help calm the mind and regulate your nervous system. With each inhale and exhale, you're syncing with the rhythm of life itself.

Scientific research confirms what we intuitively know: mindfulness practices measurably increase vagal tone and reduce stress responses. It's both ancient wisdom and modern medicine.

Another powerful tool is the **body scan**, a guided journey through your physical sensations. This practice fosters deeper awareness and reduces tension by systematically bringing attention to each area of the body. To begin, lie comfortably and close your eyes. Starting at your toes, gradually shift attention upward, observing without judgment. As you release tension, you create space for mental clarity and connection to your body's innate wisdom.

Bringing mindfulness into daily life transforms ordinary routines into moments of presence.

- Mindful eating invites you to savor each bite, improving both digestion and awareness.
- Walking meditation connects body and mind as you move in rhythm with your environment.
- Even tasks like washing dishes, folding laundry, or commuting become opportunities to pause, feel, and re-center.

Engage fully in these moments without distraction. Let them root you in the here and now.

Reflection Section: Moment-to-Moment Awareness

Carry a small notebook or use a note-taking app to jot down moments during the day when you feel fully present. What were you doing? What did it feel like? Reflect on what these experiences reveal about your ability to engage with life as it unfolds.

MEDITATIVE PRACTICES FOR IMPROVED VAGAL FUNCTION

Amid modern life's chaos, a meditation session can feel like a quiet sanctuary—an oasis of stillness in an otherwise noisy world.

Guided meditation gently leads you through states of relaxation, helping to release built-up tension and soothe the nervous system. As you follow a calming voice, your awareness begins to shift inward. You notice each breath, each bodily sensation. The cluttered noise of daily life fades into the background. In this space, the mind settles, the heart slows, and the Vagus finds a chance to reset and recalibrate.

One deeply heart-centered practice is **Loving-Kindness Meditation**, or *Metta*. This beautiful tradition fosters compassion and goodwill, beginning with yourself and gradually expanding outward.

Start by sitting comfortably and closing your eyes. Take a few deep breaths. Gently offer yourself kind wishes such as:

"May I be happy. May I be healthy. May I be peaceful."

Then, bring others into your heart—loved ones, acquaintances, even those with whom you've experienced conflict. Extend the same well-wishes to them.

"May you be safe. May you be well. May you live with ease."

As warm feelings of connection arise, the Vagus tingles happily in response and deepens your capacity for emotional regulation. The gentle repetition of loving phrases becomes soothing, centering, and healing.

Another meditative method with decades of research behind it is **Transcendental Meditation (TM)**. TM involves the silent repetition of a personal mantra—often a sound or word—used as an anchor for the mind.

Sit comfortably, close your eyes, and softly repeat your mantra for about 20 minutes. This repetition leads the mind into a quiet state of restful alertness. TM has been shown to lower stress hormones, reduce anxiety, and improve heart rate variability. The gentle rhythm of TM allows the nervous system to soften, unwind, and come back into balance.

For some, **prayer** serves a similar role—a spiritual counterpart to meditation that connects the heart and mind to something greater. Whether prayer is spoken aloud, whispered silently, or felt internally, it has the power to calm the autonomic nervous system. It reminds us we are not alone. Whether your practice is religious or spiritual, prayer can offer comfort in times of challenge.

I also developed a special practice called **Dr. Leia's Vagus Nerve Meditation**, designed specifically to support this vital nerve.

- To begin: Sit or lie comfortably. Place one hand over your heart and the other on your abdomen. Begin with slow, diaphragmatic breathing. Feel your body soften.
- Now, imagine a soft, golden light illuminating the path of your Vagus—from your brainstem, winding through your heart, lungs, diaphragm, and all the way down into your digestive system. Visualize this light gently massaging the nerve, moving up and down with your breath like a loving, internal current.
- As you breathe, silently offer gratitude for your body's incredible systems—heartbeat, breath, digestion—all functioning without your conscious effort. Feel awe for these automatic rhythms of life that keep you alive and well.

In these still moments, you reconnect with your body's wisdom. The Vagus responds to this inner reverence. Meditation becomes not only a mental exercise, but a full-body, full-spirit experience of calm.

Now, if you're thinking to yourself, *"But I can't quiet my mind for longer than three seconds! I'm like a squirrel—I'm terrible at meditating!"* don't skip over this section thinking it's not for you.

Many of my patients have said the exact same thing. And here's what I tell them:

If you struggle to slow down your mind or focus on one thing, *that's precisely why* you should practice meditation.

The moment you notice your mind wandering off to your to-do list, that awkward thing you said in 2012, or what's for dinner, that's not a failure. *That moment of awareness is the exercise.* Catching yourself and gently returning to your breath or your mantra is the mental 'muscle' you're strengthening. It's like a bicep curl for your brain!

If you meditate and find your mind is wandering, congratulations— you're doing it right!

The brain's job is to generate thoughts, just like the heart's job is to beat. It's what it does. But just because your brain creates thoughts doesn't mean you have to follow every one of them down a rabbit hole. You can step back, observe the thought, and say, *"Nope, not going there right now,"* and gently redirect your focus.

That's the real benefit of meditation: the learned ability to direct your mind where you want it to go.

If you have an overactive mind, struggle to wind down, have ADHD, or just find focusing difficult, let me assure you—meditation is 100% worth five minutes of your day. It won't just help you feel calmer; it will actually help you become more focused and productive after-ward. Think of it as a mental reset button—and who couldn't use one of those?

Mindset, in its simplest form, is the lens through which you view the world. As Jim Kwik eloquently states in his book *Limitless*, mindset is the beliefs and attitudes that shape your reality. It's the internal dialogue that dictates how you respond to challenges, perceive success, and navigate obstacles.

A **growth mindset** allows you to see setbacks not as failures, but as opportunities for learning. This perspective is transformative. It enables you to embrace change with resilience and optimism. The real magic of mindset lies in its power to redefine what you believe is possible. It becomes a crucial tool in managing stress and enhancing your overall well-being.

Cultivating a positive mindset begins with intentional self-talk and affirmations that reinforce growth. When you're faced with adversity, pause and remind yourself of past triumphs. This strengthens your belief in your ability to overcome. Or, rather than asking yourself, "What if it doesn't work out?" you could borrow Mel Robbins' phrase: "What if it all works out?"

I would go so far as to say that a positive mindset is essential for healing. Over the years, I've worked with many individuals facing chronic illness, depression, anxiety, or long-standing emotional pain. One common thread I've seen is this:

If someone doesn't believe they can get better, they rarely do.

I've asked patients to describe what a healthy, thriving version of themselves would look or feel like—and many struggled to answer. They couldn't imagine it. And if you can't see the possibility of healing, how can you move toward it?

It makes sense. Suppose you don't believe change is possible. In that case, you're less likely to seek information, ask for help, explore treatment options, engage in self-care, or invest time and energy in your well-being. Without that effort, progress doesn't happen. And then the original belief—*"See? I knew I wouldn't get better."*—gets reinforced.

This cycle doesn't just apply to health. It applies to any area of life where growth is possible: relationships, finances, organization, peace of mind—anything. It all begins with belief.

The first and most powerful step toward change is believing—*truly* believing—that it's possible.

JOURNALING AS A TOOL FOR EMOTIONAL CLARITY

Journaling is a valuable practice for gaining emotional clarity and creating space for self-reflection. When you write down your thoughts and feelings, you externalize them, transforming swirling emotions into words that can be seen, understood, and processed. It's a way of exploring how you feel and why, in a space free from judgment.

Reflective journaling acts like a mirror for your inner world, helping you recognize patterns, triggers, and deeper insights that might otherwise go unnoticed. It becomes a quiet conversation with yourself—one that invites honesty, vulnerability, and personal growth. Over time, this simple act of writing can shift your relationship with your emotions, helping you respond with greater awareness and intention.

Start with a few gentle prompts:

- How do I usually react when I feel overwhelmed or upset?
- What's one emotion I tend to avoid or suppress? Why?
- How comfortable am I sharing my feelings with others? What holds me back?
- What emotions did I experience today, and what might have triggered them?
- How did I respond to today's challenges, and what did I learn about myself?

These questions spark reflection and build **emotional intelligence** – the ability to recognize, understand, and manage your own emotions and empathize with others. As you begin to notice recurring themes—whether limiting beliefs, hidden fears, or untapped strengths—you'll gain a clearer picture of your internal landscape. That awareness is often the first step toward meaningful change.

The benefits of journaling go beyond the emotional. Research shows that expressive writing can reduce stress hormones and enhance vagal tone. The very act of organizing your thoughts onto paper brings a sense of relief, activating the parasympathetic nervous system and inviting calm. Journaling, in this way, becomes both a mental and physiological reset. Journaling offers a far more effective and healthy outlet than venting to others, which—despite common belief—often reinforces negative emotions rather than resolving them.

Different journaling techniques can support different goals. **Free writing**—setting a timer and writing whatever comes to mind without censoring yourself—can be surprisingly liberating. It often uncovers thoughts you didn't even realize were there. **Gratitude journaling**, on the other hand, trains your brain to focus on the good, shifting perspective away from stress and scarcity and toward appreciation and abundance.

There are no rules when it comes to journaling. It's your space, your voice, your pace. Whether you write a few lines a day or fill pages in a single sitting, each entry is a step toward self-discovery. Over time, these written reflections become a roadmap of your inner evolution, revealing not only where you've been but also where you're ready to go.

Journal Prompt Inspiration

Your journaling practice is a private place to release, reflect, and realign. Here are some questions to spark insight:

Emotional Awareness

- What emotion am I feeling most strongly right now? Why?
- When did I feel most at peace today?
- What drained my energy today? What restored it?

Gratitude & Positivity

- What are three small things I'm grateful for today?
- Who brought a moment of joy or kindness into my day?
- What made me smile recently?

Stress Reflection

- What's been weighing on me lately—and what might help lighten it?
- How does my body feel when I'm stressed? What soothes it?
- What's one thing I can let go of today?

Self-Discovery

- What limiting belief might be holding me back right now?
- What does my ideal day look like—and what's one step I can take toward it?
- What does my inner voice sound like today: kind, critical, calm, scattered?

Evening Wind-Down

- What did I do well today?
- What's one thing I learned or realized?
- What can I do tomorrow to support my well-being?

Guided Imagery for Emotional Balance

Guided imagery is a powerful tool for regulating the mind and emotions. This practice uses your imagination to create soothing mental landscapes—perhaps a quiet forest, a sun-dappled meadow, or the rhythmic lull of ocean waves. By engaging all your senses, you deepen your experience, grounding yourself in calm and presence.

Visualization helps reduce anxiety, elevate mood, and shift the nervous system from stress mode into a state of rest and restoration. It's like giving your mind a mini-vacation—one that's always available, no passport required.

If you're new to guided imagery, don't worry. You can find pre-recorded scripts on YouTube or meditation apps like Headspace or Calm. These often include peaceful music or nature sounds to enhance the sensory experience. As you become more familiar with the process, you might try crafting your own visual journeys. Personalize them to focus on specific goals—like inner calm, clarity, or healing—and include details like temperature, sounds, and scents to make your imagery come alive.

To get started, find a quiet, comfortable spot. Close your eyes and take a few grounding breaths. Picture a place where you feel completely at ease. Maybe it's a warm, sandy beach with waves gently lapping the shore, or a mountaintop where cool air brushes your cheeks. Feel the textures, hear the ambient sounds, and let yourself fully inhabit the space. As your body softens and your breath slows, you're teaching your nervous system how to access this calm more easily in everyday life.

Over time, guided imagery can become yet another resource in your emotional toolkit. With practice, you'll be able to call on these internal sanctuaries anytime stress, fear, or overwhelm threaten to take over.

If you find yourself feeling stuck or hitting a plateau—even after trying all your usual self-help tools—that may be your cue to seek professional support. Sometimes, a gentle nudge from a trained guide can move your personal growth forward. We all have blind spots. It can be tricky to recognize our own maladaptive mindset, especially when we're living a life shaped by it.

We may mistake a limiting belief for something normal, inevitable, or even helpful. And often, there's an inner resistance to changing ourselves, because change requires admitting that what we've been doing hasn't been working. It may even mean facing the uncomfortable possibility that some of our suffering has been self-induced. That can be a painful—but ultimately liberating—realization.

In my mind-body practice (drleiaanderson.com), I specialize in a type of Holistic Counseling method called **The Vis Dialogue.**

The Latin phrase *vis medicatrix naturae* translates as "the healing power of nature." Specifically, "vis" on its own means "the power" or "the force." The phrase dates back to Hippocrates (~400 BCE), often called the "Father of Medicine." Hippocrates observed that the body has an innate ability to heal itself — for example, wounds close, fevers resolve, and infections clear. Early physicians believed their job was not to conquer disease, but to support the body's natural healing processes. In Hippocratic thought, treatments like rest, good food, herbs, and bathing were ways to assist the vis, not override it.

In modern naturopathic medicine, *the vis* refers to the self-healing, self-regulating force within living beings. It's the vital energy or intelligence that maintains health and restores balance when disrupted.

The Vis Dialogue approach helps clients uncover their maladaptive beliefs and recognize the deep connections between their beliefs (both conscious and subconscious), thoughts, emotions, behaviors, and physical symptoms. It's a process of self-discovery—learning to see what you hadn't been aware of before.

And as the saying goes, knowledge is power. With new awareness comes the power to shift and release old patterns and choose a more intentional path that supports your mental, emotional, and physical well-being. By removing mental and emotional blocks to healing, the self-healing force – the vis – can return without as much resistance.

A Holistic Counseling Case Example

I once worked with a woman in her early 30s who told me she had been anxious for as long as she could remember. She believed it was just part of who she was—something she'd been born with and would always have to manage, but never truly resolve. Although she hated the feeling, part of her believed the anxiety was useful. She thought that by constantly imagining worst-case scenarios, she could somehow prepare herself if something bad actually happened.

Through our work together, I asked her some questions to gently challenge those beliefs:

- Is it true that you were born destined to be anxious?
- Does worrying actually prepare a person for disaster?
- Is it possible that the anxiety was learned? Perhaps at such a young age that you don't remember a time before it? (The woman told me she had a very cautious and worry-prone mother)

We also explored the idea that chronic worry doesn't make us more prepared for hardship. In fact, when challenges arise, we usually rise to the occasion in real time. Our instincts and inner resources guide us, without needing to rehearse every bad thing that *might* happen.

She realized: she had never truly considered the possibility that she didn't *have* to be anxious. That she might have a choice. That insight alone was enough for her to begin letting it go, within just two sessions.

9

ADVANCED TECHNIQUES FOR NERVOUS SYSTEM BLISS

VAGUS MASSAGE TECHNIQUES

Imagine a gentle touch that melts tension and invites a wave of calm through your entire body. That's the essence of Vagus massage techniques that tap into your body's natural healing systems. By stimulating key access points along the Vagus, these massages can reduce stress, soothe inflammation, and even improve digestion. It's simple, nurturing, and surprisingly effective.

Neck & Throat Massage: A Gentle Wake-Up Call

The Vagus runs close to the surface along the sides of your neck, making it one of the most accessible areas for massage.

To try it:

- Sit comfortably and use your fingertips to gently massage the sides of your neck in slow, circular motions.
- Move upward toward your jawline, then down toward your collarbone.

This gentle stimulation improves circulation, relieves muscle tension, and encourages the Vagus to activate its calming parasympathetic signals. Many people find it helpful for reducing tension headaches and lifting low moods.

Abdominal Massage: For Gut Health & Grounding

The gut and brain are in constant communication via the Vagus, and abdominal massage can support this dialogue.

To try it:

- Lie on your back with your knees bent.
- Use both hands to massage your abdomen in slow, clockwise circles (this follows the natural direction of your digestive tract).

This simple technique can ease bloating, support digestion, and improve vagal tone, making it beneficial for both physical and emotional well-being.

Tragus Massage: Calm in a Pinch

Need a quick hit of calm? Try this discreet technique:

- Locate the small flap of cartilage just outside your ear canal (that's the tragus).
- Gently squeeze and release it using your thumb and forefinger for about 30 seconds.

This stimulates the auricular branch of the Vagus, often producing an immediate sense of relaxation. It's perfect for moments of overwhelm or anxiety, and you can do it anytime, anywhere.

Boost Benefits with Essential Oils

Essential oils (EO) can amplify the calming effects of massage. Here are some top essential oils for relaxation and nervous system support:

- **Lavender (Lavandula angustifolia)**: One of the most studied oils for calming the nervous system. Reduces anxiety, promotes relaxation, and improves sleep. Gentle on the skin and widely used in massage blends.
- **Roman Chamomile (Chamaemelum nobile)**: Soothing to both mind and body; great for tension and irritability. Mild sedative effects; excellent for sensitive individuals.
- **Sweet Marjoram (Origanum majorana)**: Deeply calming, particularly good for muscle tension and stress. Traditionally used to ease nervous restlessness.
- **Frankincense (Boswellia carterii or sacra)**: Grounding and centering; slows and deepens the breath. Helpful when anxiety feels "unmoored" or spiritual in nature.
- **Bergamot (Citrus bergamia, bergaptene-free)**: Uplifting yet calming; balances mood swings, relieves nervous tension. Make sure to use bergaptene-free (FCF) to avoid phototoxicity when applied to skin.
- **Ylang Ylang (Cananga odorata)**: Eases tension, lowers blood pressure, and is emotionally comforting. Use sparingly; its strong scent can be overpowering in large amounts.
- **Clary Sage (Salvia sclarea)**: Calms the mind, relieves nervous tension, especially around hormonal shifts. Often used for relaxation during PMS or menopause.

Tips for Safe Topical Use of EO in Massage

- **Dilution matters!** Essential oils should always be diluted in a carrier oil (like sweet almond, jojoba, or fractionated coconut) before applying to the skin.

- **General relaxation massage**: 1–2% dilution → 5–10 drops EO per 1 ounce (30 mL) carrier oil.
- **Patch test first** for individuals who tend to have sensitive skin.
- **Avoid sensitive areas**: no application near eyes, mucous membranes, or broken skin.

Favorite Relaxation Blend Example

Here's a simple blend you can try: 4 drops Lavender, 3 drops Sweet Marjoram, 2 drops Frankincense, 1 oz carrier oil

Optional bonus: Add gentle music, a darkened room, and mindful breathing during the massage to deepen nervous system relaxation.

OTHER HANDS-ON TECHNIQUES FOR VAGAL SUPPORT

Massage isn't the only touch technique to nurture your nervous system. These additional body-based modalities also promote vagal tone and overall balance:

Reflexology

This technique applies pressure to specific points on the feet that correspond with organs and systems throughout the body. Practitioners believe stimulating these points enhances circulation, supports detoxification, and promotes full-body relaxation.

Trigger Point Release

Targeting muscle 'knots' or tight spots, this technique helps release tension that may be impeding nerve signaling. Trigger point work can improve range of motion, reduce pain, and optimize the body's communication pathways, including the Vagus.

Neuro-Fascial Release

Fascia is the connective tissue that surrounds muscles, nerves, and organs. When it becomes tight or restricted, it can disrupt nervous system function. Gentle fascial release restores flow, balance, and ease throughout the body.

Craniosacral Therapy & Cranial Release Technique

These gentle, hands-on approaches focus on the alignment and movement of cranial bones. Subtle adjustments help optimize the flow of cerebrospinal fluid and reduce restrictions that affect the nervous system. Many clients report feeling deeply relaxed, with reduced anxiety and improved sleep after just a few sessions.

Science Meets Self-Care

Massage and touch-based therapies activate the Vagus in several ways —by reducing muscle tension, lowering cortisol levels, and promoting parasympathetic activity. These shifts not only help you feel better in the moment but also support long-term resilience and healing.

Case in point: A man who had battled tension for years reported significant improvement in his sleep and a decrease in irritability after incorporating regular neck massages into his weekly routine.

Another individual experienced improved digestion and decreased bloating after practicing daily abdominal massage for just a few weeks (with a drop of castor oil applied to the navel).

These stories reflect what research is beginning to confirm: that hands-on techniques offer real, measurable support for nervous system regulation.

A Return to Inner Wisdom

Vagus massage and related techniques are also invitations to slow down and reconnect with your body's innate intelligence. As you incorporate these tools into your self-care rituals, notice how your body responds. These small, loving actions send a powerful message to your nervous system: *you are safe, supported, and healing.*

If the idea of having tiny needles gently placed in your skin doesn't exactly scream *relaxation*, give acupuncture a second look—it might just become your new favorite nervous system tune-up.

A cornerstone of Traditional Chinese Medicine (TCM), acupuncture offers a time-tested method for stimulating the Vagus and supporting overall health. Rooted in the ancient art of balancing the body's life force, or *Qi*, acupuncture involves placing fine, hair-thin needles at specific points along energy pathways known as meridians. While it may sound a bit mystical, the results are anything but—acupuncture blends the wisdom of centuries with modern neuroscience to help you feel calm, clear, and centered.

In the TCM view, health is more than just the absence of symptoms—it's a dynamic state of harmony between your body, mind, and environment. Acupuncture helps restore this harmony.

Acupuncture Meets the Vagus Nerve

So, where does the Vagus come in? Some of the acupuncture points most closely associated with vagal activation are located along nerve-rich areas like the ear, neck, and abdomen. Stimulating these points has been shown to influence the Vagus directly, especially via the auricular branch that passes through the outer ear. That means a tiny needle in just the right spot on your ear can help activate your rest-and-digest system. (Talk about small effort, big results!)

Modern science is catching up with what acupuncturists have known for centuries. Targeting these areas doesn't just help with muscle tension—it can promote nervous system balance at a deep, foundational level.

What's Actually Happening?

From a physiological perspective, acupuncture stimulates the release of feel-good neurotransmitters like serotonin and dopamine, as well as endorphins, the body's natural painkillers. This neurochemical cocktail helps reduce cortisol, elevate your mood, and ease physical discomfort. Essentially, acupuncture coaxes your body into doing what it already knows how to do—heal, regulate, and rebalance—but with a bit more encouragement.

These effects sync beautifully with the parasympathetic nervous system's goals: rest, digest, and *chill out.*

How Can It Help?

Acupuncture's benefits extend across the spectrum of vagus-connected health concerns:

- **Chronic pain relief** – Reduces inflammation and boosts circulation
- **Digestive support** – Regulates gut motility and eases bloating or constipation
- **Emotional well-being** – Helps manage anxiety, depression, and general nervous tension
- **Hormonal balance & sleep support** – Improves mood regulation and rest quality

It's like a Swiss Army knife for your nervous system: one elegant tool with a lot of versatile uses.

During my training as a naturopathic doctor at Sonoran University of Health Sciences, I was introduced to the world of TCM and acupuncture, not just from textbooks, but hands-on. In clinic rotations, I had the opportunity to administer acupuncture treatments to patients, practice on classmates (and myself!), and experience the therapy firsthand as a patient. I can confidently say: It feels fantastic.

More than that, I've witnessed just how powerful and versatile this modality can be. I've had a stubborn headache vanish mid-treatment, watched patients with sciatica walk out pain-free, and seen women struggling with infertility conceive after a series of sessions. The list of successes is long and inspiring—try it out and see what your success story turns out to be!

Choosing the Right Practitioner

If you're curious about trying acupuncture for Vagus support, the first step is finding a qualified, experienced practitioner. Look for someone certified by a reputable board, like the National Certification Commission for Acupuncture and Oriental Medicine (NCCAOM) in the U.S.

During your initial visit, don't be shy about asking questions. Share your wellness goals and inquire about the practitioner's experience treating Vagus-related concerns. A good acupuncturist will listen carefully and create a treatment plan tailored to your unique symptoms and lifestyle. They should explain what they're doing in a way that makes you feel both informed and at ease.

Safety tip: Make sure they use sterile, single-use needles—standard practice for licensed professionals, and your best defense against infection.

A Needle's-Eye View of Wellness

Acupuncture is yet another way to slow down, breathe deeply, and tune in to your body's signals. Many people walk out of their sessions feeling lighter, calmer, and more in tune with themselves.

Whether you're managing pain, easing digestive discomfort, or seeking emotional balance, acupuncture offers a gentle, holistic option. Grounded in ancient wisdom and validated by modern science, it's a practice that meets you where you are—and helps guide you back to where you want to be.

EMOTIONAL FREEDOM TECHNIQUES (EFT) FOR STRESS RELIEF

Imagine being able to calm your nerves and shift your emotional state, just by tapping on a few key points on your body. That's the idea behind **Emotional Freedom Techniques**, or EFT (a.k.a. tapping). It combines gentle acupressure with mindful self-talk, helping to reduce stress and improve Vagus function.

The process is surprisingly simple: you tap on specific acupressure points while focusing on a particular emotion or concern. The practice emerged in the 1990s through the work of psychologist Dr. Roger Callahan, and it's since become a popular self-help tool. The basic concept is this: acknowledge how you're feeling, tap gently through it, and give your nervous system a chance to reset.

To try it out, start by identifying what you're feeling—anxiety, sadness, frustration, or even physical discomfort. Accept the emotion without judgment. Then begin tapping the *karate chop point* (the meaty outer edge of your hand), while saying something like, "Even though I feel anxious, I deeply and completely accept myself."

From there, work through the following tapping points:

- Inner edge of the eyebrow
- Outer side of the eye
- Directly under the eye, on the cheekbone
- In the middle of the space between the nose and the upper lip
- Below the lower lip, in the middle of the depression at the top of the chin
- Just below the inner edge of the collarbone (this point may feel a bit tender)
- Under the armpit on the side, about level with where a bra strap would fall
- Top of the head, midline

Tap each point quickly and gently for about six to eight seconds while either repeating your setup phrase or simply staying present with what you're feeling. For more information, check out the article titled: Emotional Freedom Technique (EFT): Tap to Relieve Stress and Burnout (published in the Journal of Interprofessional Education and Practice in Jan of 2023)

EFT has been shown to reduce cortisol (your primary stress hormone), calm the nervous system, and support emotional resilience. That makes it an excellent tool for supporting vagal tone, especially during moments of acute pain or stress. I've personally seen it bring a migraine from a 10/10 pain level down to a 5 in just 15 minutes. It's especially helpful for intense emotions like panic or overwhelm, and it often works surprisingly fast.

One of the best parts? It's free, simple, and has zero side effects. If it works, great—you've got a powerful tool in your self-care kit. And if it doesn't help in the moment, you've still taken time to pause and check in with yourself, which is valuable in its own right.

EFT helps you get out of your head and back into your body in a gentle, non-invasive way. It encourages emotional honesty and nervous system regulation at the same time. Whether you're easing stress in the middle of a hectic day or working through deeper emotional patterns, tapping gives you a direct line to calming your system and supporting your overall well-being.

TRACKING YOUR PROGRESS: MEASURING VAGAL TONE

Imagine having a high-tech mirror that reflects the subtle, often invisible ways your body responds to daily life—stress, calm, focus, fatigue. That's the beauty of **biofeedback**. It turns your internal signals—like heart rate, breath, and muscle tension—into something you can see and understand in real time. This self-awareness becomes a tool for transformation, giving you a direct way to improve vagal tone and build stress resilience.

At its core, biofeedback is all about awareness. It helps you notice how your body reacts to stress (often before your brain consciously registers it), and teaches you how to shift into a calmer, more balanced state. Think of it as a nervous system tuning fork—showing you what throws you off key and helping you get back in sync.

One of the most popular and accessible forms of biofeedback is heart rate variability (HRV) monitoring. HRV measures the variation in time between heartbeats. This fascinating little metric says a lot about your autonomic nervous system. A higher HRV score generally means you're rocking a strong vagal tone and bouncing back from stress like a champ. A lower HRV might suggest your nervous system is stuck in a stress response and needs a little TLC.

Recommended Devices and Apps for HRV + Biofeedback

(Always choose based on your budget and tech preferences!)

- **Whoop** – Popular with athletes, but great for anyone focused on recovery and stress resilience
- **Oura Ring** – Discreet and stylish with solid HRV and sleep tracking
- **Heart Math Inner Balance** – Specifically designed for vagal tone and emotional regulation
- **Elite HRV** or **HRV4Training** – Great apps for data-lovers, especially when paired with a Polar H10 chest strap
- **Apple Watch** – Includes basic HRV monitoring, plus breathing prompts and mindfulness apps

There are plenty of HRV monitors on the market—wearables, chest straps, finger sensors—often paired with intuitive apps that track your data and offer insights. But using biofeedback isn't just about strapping on a device and hoping for the best. The real magic comes when you engage with the information it gives you.

Start by gathering baseline data: What's your HRV like during meditation? After a stressful Zoom call? On a walk in nature? Over time, you'll start to spot patterns. Maybe your HRV spikes when you listen to classical piano. Perhaps it drops every time you skip lunch or have a difficult conversation. These clues can help you fine-tune your habits—think of it as nervous system detective work.

From there, you can experiment with some of the interventions that support vagal health we've discussed: slow belly breathing, mindfulness meditation, posture adjustments, gentle movement, sound therapy, etc. Biofeedback shows you—objectively—what's working. That kind of instant validation can be both motivating and empowering.

And it's not just about the numbers. The act of tuning into your body, pausing to check in, and being curious about what you're observing is beneficial. With practice, the insights you gain will start to shape your daily choices—what you eat, how you breathe, when you rest—and gradually, you'll feel more grounded, balanced, and in tune with yourself.

Biofeedback is a bridge between your inner experience and outer behavior—between what your body's trying to tell you and how you respond. It helps you to be proactive about creating a life that supports your nervous system, rather than overwhelms it.

So, whether you're experimenting with gadgets or simply using a mindful breath to shift your state, you're engaging in one of the most essential skills of nervous system health: listening. Really listening. And as you've seen throughout this chapter—from massage and acupuncture to EFT and now biofeedback—there are so many ways to support vagal tone. The goal is connection – with your body, your breath, your inner wisdom – and the peace that lives there, waiting for you to return.

Beginner-Friendly Biofeedback Tips

- **Start small.** A simple HRV app with a finger sensor or smartwatch is a great intro. You don't need anything fancy!
- **Establish a baseline.** Try checking your HRV at the same time each day—first thing in the morning is ideal.
- **Note the patterns.** Track how your numbers shift with sleep, stress, movement, or meals. You'll be amazed at what you learn.
- **Don't chase the data.** Use it to guide you, not stress you out (ironically, stressing would defeat the purpose). Your body isn't a machine—it's a dynamic, living system.
- **Pair it with breathwork.** Try 5 minutes of slow breathing (inhale 4 counts, exhale 6) and see what happens to your HRV!

INTEGRATING VAGUS PRACTICES INTO DAILY LIFE

N ow here's the primary goal of this book: to take what you've learned and put it into practice. Like anything in life, you won't see results unless you take action. I didn't write this book for you to finish it, say, "Well, that's interesting," and then go right back to business as usual. I've seen that happen too many times—we all have. I want this to be your *self-help*, not just *shelf-help*!

That's why I've kept the suggestions in these chapters as efficient and straightforward as possible. My hope is that you'll not only feel inspired to try them but also stick with the ones that work for you.

And while I wish it weren't the case, in today's fast-paced world, it really is essential to carve out time for practices that support your nervous system. We have to make time for movement, especially if we have sedentary jobs. We have to read food labels, because the reality is not everything on store shelves is nourishing. In fact, some ingredients are downright harmful. And we have to prioritize rest (this was a tough lesson for me, personally), because it's all too easy to say "yes" to 18 hours of nonstop activity each day if you haven't set clear boundaries for yourself.

But here's the encouraging part: small actions truly can make a big difference—*if* you stay consistent over time. I've seen this over and over again with my clients and in my own life.

Take one patient, for example: a busy working mom who came to me completely overwhelmed by stress. Her job was too demanding, and her body was starting to bear the weight of that imbalance. Painful periods. Intense PMS depression. Joint pain. Brain fog. Weight gain. She felt like she was falling apart—and fast. But she understood when I told her that even small acts of self-care could free up more energy, sharpen her focus, and increase her capacity to handle stress with less physical toll.

So she made a plan. She started waking up just a little earlier to fit in 30 minutes of morning exercise. She set a timer at work to take a five-minute break every hour to stretch, breathe, or rest her eyes. She added a quick stretching routine and a bit of journaling before bed. And she cut out processed foods. Within a few months, all of her symptoms had significantly improved. She told me, "I feel like myself again."

Now, your plan doesn't have to look like hers. We all have different lives, different schedules, and different health priorities. The key is to find what works for *you*—and to make it your own.

DESIGNING A PERSONAL VAGUS ROUTINE

By tailoring these practices to your unique needs, you not only boost their effectiveness but also make them easier to maintain. This isn't about a massive life overhaul. It's about weaving simple, supportive habits into your everyday routine—so they feel natural, not like another item on your to-do list.

Step One: Clarify Your Goals

Start by asking yourself:

What do I want to improve?

Are you looking to reduce stress or anxiety? Support digestion? Improve sleep? Feel more grounded emotionally? Improve your metabolism? Reduce pain? Improve your energy and focus? Identifying your top priorities will help guide your choices.

Then, take a look at your current lifestyle. If mornings are chaotic, a calm evening routine might work better. If your afternoons tend to drag, that could be the perfect window for a breathwork break or short walk. The goal is to meet yourself where you are and design a realistic plan that you can actually commit to.

Step Two: Establish Your Baseline

Tune into your body. How does stress show up for you? How's your sleep, digestion, and mood? Try using an HRV monitor to get a more objective sense of how your nervous system is functioning. Having a starting point helps you track progress and notice subtle improvements along the way.

Step Three: Choose Your Tools

Think of this like building a self-care toolbox:

- **Physical practices:** Gentle yoga, stretching, or massage
- **Mental practices:** Meditation, mindfulness, breathwork, journaling
- **Lifestyle support:** Balanced nutrition, social connection, nature time

You don't need to do everything at once. Start with a couple of practices that feel doable and supportive.

Step Four: Make It Stick

Small steps work best. Set realistic starting goals and build from there. Consider habit stacking, a strategy made popular by SJ Scott and James Clear. Link a vagus-supporting practice to something you already do, like:

- Relaxing into a yoga pose while your coffee brews
- Doing a quick neck release stretch before brushing your teeth
- Pausing for a mindfulness check-in and breathing exercise between meetings

These micro-practices add up—and they're often easier to maintain than a big, time-consuming overhaul.

Reflection Section: Personal Routine Planner

Create a simple template to outline your vagus-supporting routine. Include:

- *Your wellness goals*
- *Selected practices (physical, mental, lifestyle)*
- *Time of day or habit you'll pair them with*

Example:

Goal	Practice	When
Reduce stress	4-7-8 breathing	On Waking
Improve digestion	Abdominal massage	After lunch
Fall asleep faster	Journaling & PMR	Before bed

This personalized approach transforms vague intentions into practical habits. More importantly, it makes your wellness journey feel truly your own. And that sense of ownership? It's one of the most powerful motivators there is.

BALANCING WORK AND WELLNESS: VAGAL EXERCISES FOR THE BUSY

I've had countless patients sit across from me with the very best of intentions, nodding emphatically as they say yes, they want to change their diet, make time for meditation, and practice their yoga or other exercise regularly. But too often, life gets in the way.

Let me say this clearly: *don't wait for your life to get less busy—because chances are, it won't.*

In the whirlwind of daily responsibilities, carving out time for self-care can feel like an impossible luxury. Erratic schedules, deadlines, and high-pressure environments often make wellness feel like one more thing on an already overloaded plate. If you've ever felt like juggling work, family, and health is just too much, know that you're not alone.

But here's the good news: supporting your Vagus doesn't have to be complicated or time-consuming. Many of these practices can be seamlessly woven into your daily routine—and they feel good, like taking a break rather than having more things 'to do.'

Start with simple, two-to-five-minute breathing exercises during breaks at work. These mini-pauses can have a significant impact, shifting you out of stress mode and into a more relaxed, focused state. At your desk, try gentle neck stretches or shoulder rolls that stimulate the Vagus. These movements release tension and refresh your mind— perfect for a mid-afternoon reset. I will often get up and do some stretches in my office between clients. Lunges, forward folds, side-bends, and neck rolls all help to get the blood flowing back to my brain and ease the little aches that start setting in with too much physical inactivity.

You can also shape your physical workspace to support your nervous system. Think ergonomics: adjust your chair height, explore a standing desk, or be mindful of your posture. Even subtle changes can reduce physical stress and promote better circulation, which in turn supports vagal tone.

If you're in a shared work environment, consider inviting others into the wellness conversation. Group breathing breaks or a few minutes of quiet mindfulness can become part of your office culture, encouraging connection and reducing collective stress.

And let's not forget boundaries. They're essential when you're trying to prioritize your well-being. Schedule short recharge breaks like you would a meeting, and don't be afraid to communicate your needs to colleagues or your boss. Protecting your time for wellness is not selfish—it's self-sustaining.

When life feels full to the brim, don't underestimate the power of small, consistent shifts. A few mindful minutes here, a calming breath there—they add up. As you integrate these micro-practices into your day, you'll find that even during the busiest weeks, there's still room for peace, presence, and a deeper connection with yourself.

*** Quick Vagal Boosts for Busy People ***

Top 5 Micro-Practices to Reset in Minutes

1. **60-Second Breath Break**: Inhale for 4, hold for 4, exhale for 6. Repeat for 1 minute. Instant calm, zero side effects.
2. **Desk Neck Stretch**: Tilt your head gently from side to side, then look left and right. Your neck appreciates the break – it's hard work carrying around that brain!
3. **Tragus Massage**: Gently pinch and release the small flap of cartilage in front of your ear. Stimulates the auricular branch of the Vagus—no yoga mat required.
4. **Mindful Sip**: Close your eyes while sipping herbal tea or water. Focus on the warmth, the taste, the pause. A brief moment of mindful presence.
5. **3-Minute Nature Glance**: Look out a window or step outside if you can. Gazing at trees or sky—even briefly—can soothe the nervous system.

Tip: Stack these practices with something you already do—like waiting for your tea to brew, during your commute, or after checking emails. Wellness works best when it fits your real life.

FAMILY-FRIENDLY VAGUS ACTIVITIES

Picture a bustling kitchen on a Sunday afternoon—aromas swirling, laughter echoing, everyone gathered around prepping a meal. Now imagine that this moment isn't just about food—it's also about wellness. When families integrate Vagus-friendly activities into their routines, health becomes a shared value, not a solo mission. These moments of connection deepen bonds, create lasting traditions, and turn self-care into 'us-care.'

Wellness as a Family Affair

Bringing loved ones into your wellness journey makes it easier—and more fun—to stay consistent. You're not just building habits; you're building a support system. And when the whole crew joins in, everyone benefits from a calmer, more connected home environment.

Try activities that appeal to all ages:

- **Morning family yoga** for gentle movement and breath awareness.
- **Bedtime guided meditation** as a calm, shared ritual for winding down.
- **Nature walks or 'mindful scavenger hunts'** that stimulate curiosity and conversation while promoting relaxation through rhythm and scenery.

These aren't just healthy habits—they're memories in the making.

Don't Forget the Fun Factor

Play is powerful. Joyful, spontaneous movement and laughter naturally stimulate the Vagus. Think: impromptu dance parties, backyard games, or charades. Even arts and crafts can act as calming, mindful activities that bring out everyone's creative side while lowering stress levels.

When wellness feels like fun instead of a chore, participation becomes effortless.

Parenting Stress and the Vagus: Finding Calm in the Chaos

The hustle and grind of parenting can be just as demanding—if not more so—than a high-pressure executive job. If you're feeling the stress of never catching a break… if the baby's cries and the toddler's whining are about to push you over the edge, I see you. I hear you. I've been you. (And just so you know—it *does* get easier as everyone gets older.)

Our kids can be our greatest source of joy and also our greatest source of stress. They have a special talent for pushing our buttons—often because those buttons are tied to parts of ourselves we haven't fully made peace with. And while that can be maddening, it's also one of parenting's most powerful gifts: the chance for deep personal growth.

So before you lash out, pause. Take a breath. Soften your shoulders. Acknowledge what you're feeling. (And maybe tap through a round of EFT—fast and effective!) Use these high-stress moments—when you're angry, overwhelmed, anxious, or disappointed—as cues to check in. Ask yourself: *What's really going on here?*

Is it truly about the silly putty now permanently embedded in the carpet (and if you *do* know how to get it out, please share), or is it the story you're telling yourself? Maybe it's the fear that your kids are out of control, that they'll never learn responsibility, or worse, that you're somehow failing them. In most cases, our reaction is not just about the mess—it's the meaning we've attached to it.

When we take a moment to pause, breathe, and respond to what's *actually* happening—rather than the mental spiral of catastrophizing—we shift out of fight-or-flight mode. We regulate our nervous system, and in doing so, we become more present, more grounded, and ultimately, better parents.

If you're looking for more inspiration, I highly recommend the work of Dr. Shefali Tsabary. Her books on mindful parenting are insightful, compassionate, and often exactly what overwhelmed parents need to hear.

Creating a Sustainable Routine

Make wellness time a regular part of your family schedule—whether it's Sunday stretch sessions or Friday evening breathing breaks. Give everyone a voice in what you do, so each person feels included and heard. This shared planning not only boosts engagement but also fosters a sense of responsibility and encourages participation.

By anchoring these practices into your family rhythm, you're nurturing an environment that values health, joy, and connection. Wellness becomes part of your family culture—something you do together, grow through together, and carry forward for generations.

*** Vagus Activities by Age ***

Simple ways to help kids (and kids at heart) relax, reset, and reconnect

For Littles (Ages 3–7):

- **Bubble Breathing:** Blow slow, steady bubbles to practice straw breathing
- **Teddy Bear Belly Breaths:** Lie down with a stuffed animal on the tummy and watch it rise and fall to practice diaphragmatic breathing
- **Animal Yoga:** Try lion's breath, cat-cow, or butterfly pose— bonus points for sound effects!

For Big Kids (Ages 8–12):

- **Mindful Coloring:** Calm the mind with mandalas or nature-themed pages.
- **Laugh Games:** Try 'laugh yoga'—intentionally giggling until it becomes real laughter.
- **Nature Detective Walks:** Collect leaves, identify sounds, or create nature art from found treasures.

For Teens (Ages 13+):

- **Box Breathing:** Inhale for 4, hold for 4, exhale for 4, hold for 4. Great before tests or sleep.
- **Music + Movement:** Create a playlist of calming or upbeat songs to dance, stretch, or chill out.
- **Guided Visualization:** Use meditation apps or recordings to build emotional awareness and calm the mind.

Tip: Keep it light! Let your child lead or choose the activity when possible—it's more effective (and enjoyable) when they feel in control.

MORNING RITUALS FOR OPTIMAL VAGAL ACTIVATION

Imagine your morning as a canvas, waiting for the first strokes of calm and focus to set the tone for your day. Establishing a morning routine that activates the Vagus can transform how you approach the challenges that lie ahead. By initiating your day with practices that engage this nerve, you create a foundation of serenity and preparedness. This process helps establish a clear mindset, allowing you to tackle tasks with poise and clarity.

Start by incorporating gentle movement. A few minutes of light stretching or yoga can help wake up the body while engaging the Vagus through breath and posture, promoting circulation and reducing tension. Pair this with breathing exercises—slow, deliberate breaths that energize and center you. As you inhale deeply, feel the rush of oxygen invigorating your senses; as you exhale, release any lingering tension. This rhythmic breathing encourages a sense of balance, preparing you for the demands of the day.

If you prefer more intense or longer morning workouts, conclude with a few minutes of stretching to cool down and some mindful breathing. What works best for me is a promise to myself to do at least 5 minutes of yoga-pilates fusion every morning. Most mornings I do 10-20 minutes, but when I'm really short on time, I can always squeeze in 5 minutes. I really feel the difference in my body and mind afterward – the kinks from sleep are worked out, I'm more awake, and I feel like I have more to give to others after I gave a little attention to myself.

Adding a moment of mindfulness can make a big difference. Spend a moment visualizing your day—a successful meeting, a peaceful commute, or simply feeling content. Try setting an intention for your day—something grounding, like "I move through today with ease," or "I am open to connection and peace." Visualize yourself navigating the day with confidence and calm. A few minutes of meditation, repeating affirmations, or simply practicing gratitude can shift your emotional tone and bring your focus to what truly matters.

The key to keeping this ritual consistent? Make it easy. Prep the night before: lay out your yoga mat, cue up your favorite meditation app, or write down a few affirmations to glance at while sipping your tea. This reduces decision fatigue in the morning, making it easier to commit to your routine. And do your best to resist the morning scroll —skipping screens (at least for the first hour if possible) helps protect your nervous system from an early jolt of stress.

These habits don't need to be elaborate or time-consuming. Even five or ten minutes of mindful movement, breathwork, or stillness can transform your mornings. As these rituals become part of your rhythm, you may find yourself moving through the day with more clarity, energy, and ease. This is your time—a chance to reconnect with yourself before the world starts asking for your attention. Protect it, cherish it, and let it be time well spent.

Morning Ritual Inspiration: Three Easy Vagus-Activating Routines

1. The 5-Minute Reset *(For the "I hit snooze twice" kind of morning)*

- 2 minutes of diaphragmatic breathing (inhale 4, exhale 6)
- 1-minute gratitude reflection (name 3 things you're grateful for)
- 2 minutes of neck and shoulder stretches

2. The Mindful Start *(Perfect for a quiet, centered morning)*

- Light yoga or stretching (Sun Salutations or Cat-Cow)
- Guided 5-minute meditation (use an app like Insight Timer or Calm)
- Affirmation of the day: "I begin my day with peace and purpose."

3. The Energizer Blend *(For mornings that need a boost without the jitters)*

- Cold plunge or an invigorating cold shower
- Uplifting music or nature sounds while getting dressed
- A brisk walk outside or 3 minutes of bouncing/rebounding to stimulate lymph and vagal tone

EVENING WIND-DOWN TECHNIQUES TO ENHANCE VAGAL TONE

As dusk descends, the transition from the day's hustle to a restful evening becomes crucial for preparing both body and mind for rejuvenation. Our evenings should not be a mindless drift into sleep while watching a TV show, but a conscious easing into tranquility. This shift signifies more than relaxation; it's about shedding stress accumulated over the day, allowing you to settle into a state of peace and recovery. Creating an evening routine that supports this transition can be just what the doctor ordered.

One effective way to prepare for sleep is through calming practices like gentle stretching or tai chi. These movements encourage a release of tension, soothing both muscles and mind. Progressive muscle relaxation (PMR) can also be a game-changer, guiding you to consciously tense and then relax each muscle group, which in turn eases stress and invites calm (revisit Chapter 4 for a refresher). Complementing these practices, sipping on relaxation teas infused with chamomile or lavender can enhance the soothing effect, while aromatherapy with calming scents creates an inviting atmosphere.

Reflection becomes a gentle companion in the evening, guiding thoughts away from the day's chaos towards peace. Journaling can act as a reflective canvas where you paint your thoughts, helping process the day's events. This practice promotes emotional closure, leaving you at peace with the day's experiences. Gratitude exercises take this further, allowing you to end the day on a positive note by acknowledging what went well. This not only fosters emotional contentment but also enhances sleep quality.

Creating a relaxing environment sets the stage for these practices. Dimming lights mimics the natural setting sun, signaling your body to wind down. Reducing noise minimizes distractions, helping you focus inward. Establishing a soothing bedtime ritual—like reading or listening to gentle music—provides a comforting routine that your body recognizes as preparation for sleep. Personalizing this environment with soft bedding or warm lighting adds another layer of comfort, inviting relaxation into every corner of your space.

Incorporating these evening wind-down techniques can create a sanctuary of calmness, allowing you to enter sleep with ease and wake up refreshed. By consciously transitioning from activity to rest, you not only enhance your vagal tone but also create a foundation for restorative sleep and rejuvenation.

Evening Ritual Inspiration: 3 Easy Relaxing Routines

1. The Gentle Unwind (15-20 minutes)

- Brew a cup of chamomile or lemon balm tea
- Dim the lights and play soft instrumental music
- Do 5–10 minutes of gentle stretching or yoga
- End with 5 minutes of diaphragmatic breathing in bed

2. Reflect + Release (30-60 minutes)

- Take a warm shower or bath with lavender essential oil
- Light a candle and journal about your day
- Write down 3 things you're grateful for
- Read a few pages of an uplifting book before sleep

3. Tech-Free Tranquility (10-15 minutes)

- Turn off screens an hour before bed
- Use a diffuser with calming oils like sandalwood or bergamot
- Practice progressive muscle relaxation while lying in bed
- Visualize a peaceful place or listen to a guided sleep meditation

Overcoming Common Barriers to Consistency

Life has a habit of tossing curveballs just when we're getting into a good rhythm. Whether it's a time crunch, a dip in motivation, or unexpected stressors, even the most well-intentioned wellness routines can get derailed. Maybe you've experienced this firsthand—travel, a family emergency, an illness, or a particularly hectic work week throws you off course, and suddenly your routine feels like a distant memory. The first step in regaining your footing? Acknowledge the challenge, without judgment. There is nothing gained from feeling guilty about falling off track.

One helpful strategy is to set goals that are both meaningful and realistic. The **SMART framework**—Specific, Measurable, Achievable, Relevant, and Time-bound—can be a powerful tool for turning vague intentions into actionable steps. Breaking big aspirations into small, attainable goals keeps progress tangible and helps build momentum. Each small success becomes fuel for the next.

Staying consistent is also easier when you're not doing it alone. Celebrate your wins, even the small ones. Did you get through your five-minute breathing practice three days in a row? That's worth a high-five. Involving friends, family, or joining a supportive wellness community can boost motivation and keep you accountable. Whether it's a group challenge or simply checking in with a buddy, shared commitment makes the journey feel less lonely and much more fun.

Flexibility is key when life gets unpredictable. Give yourself permission to scale back when needed. Even a two-minute vagal exercise counts and is far better than doing nothing at all. Variety also keeps things fresh—try switching up your techniques or experimenting with new ones to keep your routine engaging. And remember, setbacks are not failures. They're opportunities to pause, learn, and recalibrate.

When you hit a plateau or fall off track, take a moment to reflect. What changed? What got in the way? And how might you adjust your approach next time? Revisit your 'why'—the deeper reason these practices matter to you. That sense of purpose will help reignite your motivation and remind you that (as I've said before, because I want to hammer the point home) progress comes from consistency, *not* perfection. It's about showing up for yourself, again and again, in ways that feel doable, flexible, and empowering.

CONCLUSION

THE BEGINNING OF SOMETHING BEAUTIFUL

I want to offer a heartfelt thank you—for showing up for yourself, for being curious, and for making the time to explore what's possible when you reconnect with your body's innate wisdom.

Writing this book has been a labor of love—both a professional offering and a personal story. My greatest hope is that within these pages, you've found not only information but inspiration. Not just tools, but tangible hope. And not a list of things you *should* do, but a collection of practices you *want* to try—because they feel good, they make sense, and they meet you exactly where you are.

Throughout this book, we've explored the Vagus Nerve as more than just a structure in your body—it's a lifeline. A quiet force working behind the scenes, ready to guide you toward balance, vitality, and inner calm. From deep breathing and cold exposure to gentle stretching and joyful movement... from mindful meals to heartfelt connection... we've looked at simple ways to turn the volume down on stress and turn the light back on in your body, mind, and spirit.

If there's one thing I've learned over the years, it's that healing is not linear. It doesn't always look like progress. Sometimes it looks like a nap. Sometimes it looks like setting a boundary, crying in the car, or choosing to say "no" so you can say "yes" to your peace. But no matter what it looks like, your small daily choices matter. They add up.

One moment of stillness. One nourishing meal. One breath. One stretch. One brave decision to keep going.

That's how we heal.

And while it's true that life can be messy and overwhelming and full of unknowns, it's equally true that you are capable, resourceful, and deeply resilient. The inner wisdom that helped you find this book is the same wisdom that will continue to lead you forward.

So as you close this chapter (literally), I invite you to carry forward the practices that spoke to you most. Keep them close. Let them evolve. Let your routine bend and shift with the seasons of your life. Let it be gentle. Let it be yours.

And when you fall off track (because we all do), just come back. No guilt, no shame. This is not about perfection—it's about presence.

And here's the thing: when you care for your nervous system, you don't just change how you feel—you change how you show up in the world. You become more patient with your kids, more loving in your relationships, more present in your work, and more joyful in your moments. The ripple effect is real. Your healing heals more than just you.

So stay curious. Stay compassionate with yourself. Keep listening to your body and honoring what it asks for.

And above all, trust that the healing process is unfolding exactly as it's meant to.

It has been a true honor to walk this path with you.

May you move forward feeling grounded, empowered, and gently held by the quiet strength within you.

May your days be full of breath, of beauty, and of brave, small steps toward wholeness.

With love,

Dr. Leia

KEEPING THE HEALING GOING

Now that you've learned how to calm your nervous system, support your health naturally, and reconnect with your body's innate wisdom, it's time to help others find their way to the same kind of healing.

By sharing your honest review of this book on Amazon, you help other readers—just like you—discover practical, natural solutions for stress, chronic illness, emotional overwhelm, and burnout. Whether they're brand new to holistic wellness or searching for something deeper, your words can help guide them.

This book is part of a growing movement to shift health care from symptom management to true, whole-person healing. That movement grows stronger every time someone shares what worked for them.

Thank you for keeping the message alive. Vagal health—and the ripple effects it creates—stays alive when we pass on what we've learned.

Simply go to the link below:

www.amazon.com/review/review-your-purchases/?asin= B0FJQGF2X6

With Deep Appreciation,

Dr. Leia

ABOUT THE AUTHOR

Dr. Leia Anderson, ND, MS, VDP, is a licensed Naturopathic Physician and certified Vis Dialogue Practitioner with a passion for helping people heal naturally and reclaim vibrant health. With a Doctorate in Naturopathic Medicine from Sonoran University of Health Sciences and a Master's in Genetic Counseling from the University of Pittsburgh, she brings a unique blend of rigorous science and compassionate, whole-person care to her work. She also holds a BA in Microbiology with a minor in Psychology from Ohio Wesleyan University.

In private practice since 2013, Dr. Leia specializes in addressing the root causes of chronic illness through a unique method of Holistic Counseling that honors the mind-body connection. Find out more at drleiaanderson.com

When she's not working with patients or writing about holistic wellness, you'll find her living the lifestyle she teaches—nourishing her family with whole foods, keeping up with her kids' adventures in sports and music, and finding joy in Pilates, mindfulness, and occasional battles with garden bugs.

Dr. Leia is an active member of the Pennsylvania Association of Naturopathic Physicians and a dedicated advocate for holistic health in her community and beyond.

REFERENCES

- Medscape. (n.d.). *Vagus nerve anatomy: Overview, gross.* https://emedicine.medscape.com/article/1875813-overview
- Cleveland Clinic. (n.d.). *Vagus nerve: What it is, function, location & conditions.* https://my.clevelandclinic.org/health/body/22279-vagus-nerve
- Massachusetts General Hospital. (n.d.). *The vagus nerve: A key player in your health and well-being.* https://www.massgeneral.org/news/article/vagus-nerve
- Top Doctors. (n.d.). *Vagus nerve dysfunction: Its main causes and symptoms.* https://www.topdoctors.co.uk/medical-articles/vagus-nerve-dysfunction-what-is-it-and-what-are-the-main-symptoms
- Badran, B. W., et al. (2015). Targeting plasticity with vagus nerve stimulation to treat psychiatric and neurological disorders. *Brain Stimulation, 8*(6), 1188–1190. https://pmc.ncbi.nlm.nih.gov/articles/PMC4615598/
- Mayo Clinic. (n.d.). *Vagus nerve stimulation clinical trials.* https://www.mayo.edu/research/clinical-trials/tests-procedures/vagus-nerve-stimulation/
- Mindd Foundation. (n.d.). *The many benefits of vagus nerve stimulation.* https://mindd.org/article/vagus-nerve-stimulation-many-benefits/
- Bauer, S., Baier, H., & Seeber, B. (2022). Clinical perspectives on vagus nerve stimulation. *Frontiers in Neuroscience, 16*, Article 9093220. https://pmc.ncbi.nlm.nih.gov/articles/PMC9093220/
- Cleveland Clinic. (n.d.). Diaphragmatic breathing exercises & benefits. *Cleveland Clinic.* https://my.clevelandclinic.org/health/articles/9445-diaphragmatic-breathing
- Huttunen, P., Rintamäki, H., & Hirvonen, J. (2024). The effects of cold exposure (cold water immersion, whole body cryotherapy) on stress. *Progress in Neuro-Psychopharmacology & Biological Psychiatry, 132*, 110075. https://www.sciencedirect.com/science/article/abs/pii/S0306456524000755
- Sound Travels. (n.d.). Sound therapy and the vagus nerve. *Sound Travels.* https://www.soundtravels.co.uk/a-Sound_Therapy_and_the_Vagus_Nerve-3617.aspx
- Bretherton, B., Atkinson, L., Murray, A., Clancy, J., Deuchars, S. A., & Deuchars, J. (2022). Transcutaneous vagus nerve stimulation could improve health outcomes. *Frontiers in Psychology, 13*, Article 9599790. https://pmc.ncbi.nlm.nih.gov/articles/PMC9599790/
- WebMD. (n.d.). Progressive muscle relaxation for stress and insomnia. *WebMD.* https://www.webmd.com/sleep-disorders/muscle-relaxation-for-stress-insomnia
- Zaccaro, A., Piarulli, A., Laurino, M., Garbella, E., Menicucci, D., Neri, B., & Gemignani, A. (2018). Self-regulation of breathing as an adjunctive treatment

of insomnia. *Frontiers in Psychiatry, 9*, Article 780. https://www.frontiersin.
org/journals/psychiatry/articles/10.3389/fpsyt.2018.00780/full

- Ruscio, M. (n.d.). Vagus nerve diet: What to eat for healthy vagal tone. *Dr.
Ruscio*. https://drruscio.com/vagus-nerve-diet/
- YogaUOnline. (n.d.). 6 vagus nerve exercises to boost your well-being.
YogaUOnline. https://yogauonline.com/yoga-practice-teaching-tips/yoga-
practice-tips/6-ways-to-stimulate-your-vagus-nerve-with-yoga-and-
breathing/
- Parsley Health. (n.d.). 8 vagus nerve stimulation exercises that help you relax.
Parsley Health. https://www.parsleyhealth.com/blog/how-to-stimulate-vagus-
nerve-exercises/
- Schwartz, A. (n.d.). The vagus nerve and eye movements: Tools for trauma
recovery. *Dr. Arielle Schwartz*. https://drarielleschwartz.com/the-vagus-nerve-
and-eye-movements-tools-for-trauma-recovery-dr-arielle-schwartz/
- Bonaz, B., Bazin, T., & Pellissier, S. (2018). The vagus nerve at the interface of
the microbiota-gut-brain axis. *Frontiers in Neuroscience, 12*, Article 49. https://
www.frontiersin.org/journals/neuroscience/articles/10.3389/fnins.2018.
00049/full
- Messaoudi, M., Lalonde, R., Violle, N., Javelot, H., Desor, D., Nejdi, A., ... &
Cazaubiel, M. (2011). Assessment of psychotropic-like properties of a
probiotic formulation (Lactobacillus helveticus R0052 and Bifidobacterium
longum R0175) in rats and human subjects. *British Journal of Nutrition, 105*(5),
755–764. https://pmc.ncbi.nlm.nih.gov/articles/PMC5056568/
- Hansen, M. M., Jones, R., & Tocchini, K. (2017). Shinrin-yoku (forest bathing)
and nature therapy: A state-of-the-art review. *International Journal of
Environmental Research and Public Health, 14*(8), 851. https://www.
sciencedirect.com/science/article/abs/pii/S0965229920305446
- Kondo, M. (2014). *The life-changing magic of tidying up: The Japanese art of
decluttering and organizing*. Ten Speed Press.
- Canadian Psychological Association. (n.d.). "Psychology Works" fact sheet:
Benefits of nature exposure. *Canadian Psychological Association*. https://cpa.ca/
psychology-works-fact-sheet-benefits-of-nature-exposure/
- Japan National Tourism Organization. (n.d.). Forest bathing in Japan (Shinrin-
yoku) | Guide. *Japan Travel*. https://www.japan.travel/en/guide/forest-
bathing/
- PositivePsychology.com. (n.d.). 18 polyvagal theory exercises & how to use
them in therapy. *PositivePsychology.com*. https://positivepsychology.com/
polyvagal-theory/
- Cleveland Clinic. (n.d.). 5 ways to stimulate your vagus nerve. *Cleveland Clinic
Health Essentials*. https://health.clevelandclinic.org/vagus-nerve-stimulation
- Kwik, J. (2020). *Limitless: Upgrade your brain, learn anything faster, and unlock
your exceptional life*. Hay House.
- Choosing Therapy. (n.d.). Guided imagery meditation for anxiety. *Choosing
Therapy*. https://www.choosingtherapy.com/guided-imagery-for-anxiety/

- Stress & Development Lab. (n.d.). Mindfulness apps. *Harvard University*. https://sdlab.fas.harvard.edu/mindfulness-apps
- Brighten, J. (n.d.). Vagus nerve massage: How to stimulate the vagus nerve. *Dr. Jolene Brighten*. https://drbrighten.com/vagus-nerve-massage/#:~:text= Stimulation%20of%20the%20vagus%20nerve,organs%20and%20influencing% 20neurotransmitter%20activity.
- Babygirija, R., Sood, M., Kannampalli, P., Sengupta, J. N., & Miranda, A. (2020). Acupuncture at the auricular branch of the vagus nerve modulates gastric motility: A study in rats. *Heliyon, 6*(11), e05049. https://www. sciencedirect.com/science/article/pii/S2666501820300738
- Koopman, F. A., Chavan, S. S., Miljko, S., Grazio, S., Sokolovic, S., Schuurman, P. R., Mehta, A. D., Levine, Y. A., Faltys, M., Zitnik, R., Tracey, K. J., & Tak, P. P. (2016). Vagus nerve stimulation inhibits cytokine production and attenuates disease severity in rheumatoid arthritis. *Proceedings of the National Academy of Sciences of the United States of America, 113*(29), 8284–8289. https://doi.org/10. 1073/pnas.1605635113
- Shao, P., Li, H., Jiang, J., Guan, Y., Chen, X., & Wang, Y. (2023). Role of vagus nerve stimulation in the treatment of chronic pain. *Neuroimmunomodulation, 30*(1), 167–183. https://doi.org/10.1159/000531626
- Breit, S., Kupferberg, A., Rogler, G., & Hasler, G. (2018). Vagus nerve as modulator of the brain–gut axis in psychiatric and inflammatory disorders. *Frontiers in Psychiatry, 9*, Article 44. https://doi.org/10.3389/fpsyt.2018.00044
- IFC Counseling. (n.d.). Using neuroscience to help calm your child. *IFC Counseling*. https://ifccounseling.com/blog/using-neuroscience-to-help-calm-your-child/
- Cedars-Sinai. (n.d.). Bolster your brain by stimulating the vagus nerve. *Cedars-Sinai Blog*. https://www.cedars-sinai.org/blog/stimulating-the-vagus-nerve. html#:~:text=Just%20a%20few%20minutes%20of,pressure%20levels%2C% E2%80%9D%20said%20Gonzales.
- Nutrition Genome. (n.d.). *How your genes affect the vagus nerve and stress response*. Retrieved July 12, 2025, from https://nutritiongenome.com/how-your-genes-affect-the-vagus-nerve-and-stress-response/
- Austelle, C. W., Cox, S. S., Wills, K. E., & Badran, B. W. (2024). Vagus nerve stimulation (VNS): Recent advances and future directions. *Clinical Autonomic Research, 34*(6), 529–547. https://doi.org/10.1007/s10286-024-01065-w
- Chen, M., Yang, C., Chen, Y., Nie, K., Wang, T., & Qu, Y. (2024). Research hotspots and trends of non-invasive vagus nerve stimulation: A bibliometric analysis from 2004 to 2023. *Frontiers in Neurology, 15*, Article 1429506. https://doi.org/10.3389/fneur.2024.1429506
- Mental Overstimulation: Causes, Effects, and Coping Strategies. https:// neurolaunch.com/mental-overstimulation/
- Oxford Medical Case Reports. (2025). *Oxford Medical Case Reports, 2025*(5), omaf049. https://doi.org/10.1093/omcr/omaf049
- National Library of Medicine. (n.d.). *PubMed Central (PMC)*. U.S. National Institutes of Health. https://pmc.ncbi.nlm.nih.gov/

- Khouv, A. (2017). Great vibes. Women's Fitness, (161), 40-43.
- Clear, J. (2018). *Atomic habits: An easy & proven way to build good habits & break bad ones*. Avery.
- Robbins, M. (2023, September 28). *6 magic words that stop anxiety & overwhelm (Episode 105)* [Transcript, audio, and show notes]. *Mel Robbins Podcast*. https://www.melrobbins.com/episode/episode-105/
- Daniel-Block, M. (2016). *Holistic counseling: Introducing the vis dialogue*. Balboa Press.
- National Certification Commission for Acupuncture and Oriental Medicine. (n.d.). *NCCAOM*. Retrieved July 12, 2025, from https://www.nccaom.org/
- Blacher, S. (2023). Emotional Freedom Technique (EFT): Tap to relieve stress and burnout. *Journal of Interprofessional Education & Practice, 30*, 100599. https://doi.org/10.1016/j.xjep.2023.100599